Planning on getting ahead? You'll find the business savvy you need in

CRASH COUR

- Sixteen Signs That Your Job Could Be in Trouble
- Six Ways to Implement Corporate Change
- Seventeen Factors That Make a Job Powerful
- Seven Guidelines for Naming a Product
- Nine Ways to Get the Most out of Conventions
- Six Reasons Businessmen Act Unethically
- Eleven Events That May Trigger a Unionizing Drive
- Thirty-seven Business Handbooks
- What Happens As a Company Grows
- How to Train a Successor
- Thirteen Ways to Attract Good People to Your Company
- Twelve Essentials for Good Presentations
- Seven Managerial Qualities and How They Are Assessed
- Six Professional Pitfalls
- The Five Stages of a Corporate Turnaround
- Thirty Negotiating Tactics
- Eight Power Indicators
- How Top Management Differs from Middle Management and Everyone Else
- The Five Steps in Learning to Love Corporations
- Ten Tactics to Use When the Safety of Your Product Is Questioned

CRASH COURSE

The Instant M.B.A.

Suzanne Lainson

FAWCETT CREST • NEW YORK

Library of Congress Catalog Card Number: 83-9526
ISBN 0-449-20949-0
This edition published by arrangement with G. P. Putnam's Sons/
A Stonesong Press Book

Manufactured in the United States of America

First Ballantine Books Edition: May 1986

The author gratefully acknowledges permission from the following to reprint material in their control:

Administrative Science Quarterly for material from "Building Organizational Commitment" by Bruce Buchanan, December 1974, copyright © 1974 by Cornell University; and from "Coping with Cupid" by Robert E. Quinn, March 1977, copyright © 1977 by Cornell University.

American Association of Individual Investors for "Ten Don'ts for the Individual Investor."

American Management Associations for material from *The Failure of Success*, edited by Alfred J. Marrow, © 1972 by AMACOM; from *Managing with Style and Making It Work for You* by Henry O. Golightly, © 1977 by AMACOM; "Adolescence in Organization Growth" by George Strauss in *Organization Dynamics*, Spring 1974, © 1974 by AMACOM; and from *Preventive Labor Relations* by John G. Kilgour, © 1981 by AMACOM. All rights reserved.

Mrs. Ruth A. Binstock for material from *The Road to Successful Living* by Louis Binstock, copyright © 1958 by Louis Binstock, published by Simon and Schuster.

Edward C. Bursk for material from "How to Beat the Stock Market—in the 1600s" by Joseph de la Vega, in *The World of Business*, Volume II, edited by Edward C. Bursk, Donald T. Clark, and Ralph W. Hidy, copyright © 1962 by Simon and Schuster, Inc.

The Center for Family Business for material from *Outside Directors in the Family Owned Business* by Leon A. Danco and Donald J. Jonovic, copyright © 1981 by The University Press, Inc.

Committee for Economic Development for material from *Measuring Business's Social Performance: The Corporate Social Audit* by John J. Corson and George Steiner, © 1974 by Committee for Economic Development.

Decisions Publications Inc. for material from "The New Six in Media Research" in *Media Decision*, May 1973, © 1973 by Decisions Publications Inc.

Jon English and Anthony R. Marchione for material from "Nine Steps in Management Development" by Jon English and Anthony R. Marchione in *Business Horizons*, copyright © 1977 by Foundation for the School of Business, Indiana University.

Fortune magazine for material from "The Executive Assistant" by Walter

*To G.B.F., Jr.,
who came up with the idea,
and to my family*

Contents

Preface

In the four years I spent in college studying economics and business administration I learned two things: that money should always seek the highest rate of return and that liberals who don't understand business don't win many arguments.

I was lucky to have learned so much.

In the years I've spent as a self-employed professional I've learned considerably more, a good deal of which is included in this book. For example: high-ranking executives are extremely accessible if you know how to approach them; your personality can make or break your career; and graduation from the right school will get you only so far.

Formal education has never been a prerequisite or a guarantee of business success, just as formal training has never ensured success on the battlefield. The demands of the marketplace are rarely those of academia. Many of us learn only what we have to learn when we have to learn it and then pick up our business knowledge as we need it. What we need to know at eighteen when serious job-hunting seems far in the future is much different from what we need to know when we have just assumed managerial responsibilities. We may attend the same classes, read the same books and newspapers, and watch the same television shows, but we will absorb different ideas and bits of information.

The trick, of course, is to use this selectivity to our advantage; not to spend money on a class when a book will do and not to expect from a book what only a class can provide, not to waste time with information we don't want to learn and not to miss an opportunity when we need to know. As with any endeavor that is pursued in stages and reached in levels, knowledge must be acquired at the right time to do the most good.

Unfortunately, business information is often released as it is discovered, and in the form most convenient and profitable for its originator, not in the manner most suitable for the user. Therefore, each year libraries fill up with books and periodicals that most businessmen and women have no time to read, courses are offered that don't result in discernible benefits, and strategies are initiated but falter because of lack of feedback.

Realizing that there is far more business information being generated than any one person can possibly absorb or would want to, and that few people have the time to sort out the relevant from the irrelevant, I spent hundreds of hours reading books, periodicals, and newspapers, looking for some of the most noteworthy material to include in this volume. My criteria were as follows:

1. On the assumption that much of what is taught in school either fails to register with most students or is soon forgotten, I have devoted part of this book to basic business and economic concepts that we all should know, would like to know, or are embarrassed to admit we don't know.

2. On the assumption that those of us currently in business want practical, easy-to-understand information to help and guide us in our work and lifestyle, I have devoted part of this book to useful tips, suggestions, and how-to summaries.

3. On the assumption that those of us in business also need and want motivation and inspiration, I have devoted part of this book to uplifting ideas, thought-provoking quotations, and stimulating concepts.

4. Finally, on the assumption that business can be as entertaining and fascinating as sports, television trivia, and world records, I have devoted part of this book to unusual statistics, revealing comparisons, and unexpected facts.

But by intention this book is not rigidly organized along those lines because the juxtaposition of different types of information results in a livelier and more insightful book. A synergistic effect, I hope, will take place, and one idea will lead to another.

Therefore the best way to use this book is not to begin at the beginning and read straight through to the end, but to pick a spot at random, read a few pages at a time, and repeat the process whenever you have a few minutes. Think of it as a businessperson's *I Ching*. The book is not meant to be all-inclusive (an encyclopedia is for that), but rather an appetizer—a place to start.

The list format has been used throughout because, for the busy reader, it is the more organized and readable form. Instead of wading through pages of extraneous matter, a businessman or woman can quickly scan a page and pick up the essence of any topic covered. In addition, numbered ideas are much easier to refer to and retrieve than ideas written out in paragraph form.

Very little material is directed solely to either the businessman or the businesswoman (although for convenience and readability I have used masculine pronouns more often than not). While each sex may have unique problems within a business setting, I find that much that is written specifically to one or the other underestimates the sophistication of the reader. The best business information and advice seem to be given out without regard to gender.

The purpose of this book is to educate, inform, and entertain. It will be worthwhile to anyone interested in business, no matter how experienced or new to the field. A wide variety of material has been included, demonstrating the vast amount of knowledge a businessperson has access to and may need to know; as a result, every reader should be able to learn something he or she didn't know, will be glad to know, and can use.

SUZANNE LAINSON

1

SOME BASICS

Short and Simple Sources, Facts, and Concepts

Henry Fayol's General Principles of Management

Henry Fayol, a French mining engineer, is known as the father of modern management theory and first set forth these ideas in 1916 in his book General and Industrial Management.

1. *"Division of Work."* Specialization of work leads to greater efficiency.

2. *"Authority and Responsibility."* The manager who has the "right to give orders" is at the same time responsible for his actions.

3. *"Discipline."* It is "absolutely essential for the smooth running of business and . . . without [it] no enterprise could prosper."

4. *"Unity of Command."* Each employee should have only one boss.

5. *"Unity of Direction."* All activities sharing the same objective should be directed by only one manager and one plan.

6. *"Subordination of Individual Interest to General Interest."* Organizational goals take precedence over individual ones.

3

7. *"Remuneration of Personnel."* Payment can be in a variety of forms, but "it should be fair and, as far as possible, afford satisfaction both to personnel and firm."

8. *"Centralization."* The proper amount of centralization is that which gives "the best overall yield."

9. *"Scalar Chain."* Rigid adherence to communication solely along the chain of command can be detrimental to business.

10. *"Order."* The business will run much more efficiently if there is a proper place for everything and everyone.

11. *"Equity."* Personnel should be treated with a "combination of kindliness and justice."

12. *"Stability of Tenure of Personnel."* Frequent turnover and job changes are unsettling both to employees and to the organization.

13. *"Initiative."* Employees will perform better when granted the opportunity to use their initiative.

14. *"Esprit de Corps."* Employees should be allowed to work together as a team and to communicate with each other verbally.

The Top Five Undergraduate Schools Attended by Top Executives

Based on a survey of 67,000 executives in some 38,000 public and privately held companies with sales of at least $1 million a year, conducted by Standard & Poor's, a McGraw-Hill, Inc., subsidiary.

1. Yale: 1,679.

2. Harvard: 1,366.

3. City University of New York: 1,258.

4. Princeton: 1,199.

5. New York University: 1,093.

The Top Six Graduate Schools Attended by Top Female Managers

Based on a survey of 300 senior management women in large companies, conducted by Korn-Ferry International, an executive search firm.

1. New York University: 20 percent.

2. The University of Chicago: 12.9 percent.

3. Columbia University: 10.6 percent.

4. The University of Michigan: 5.9 percent.

5. The University of Colorado: 5.9 percent.

6. Harvard: 5.9 percent.

The Top Six Graduate Schools Attended by Top Male Managers

Based on a survey conducted by Korn-Ferry International of 1,700 men in senior management in large companies.

1. Harvard: 19.5 percent.

2. New York University: 8.5 percent.

3. The University of Michigan: 5.9 percent.

4. The University of Chicago: 5.5 percent.

5. Stanford: 4.7 percent.

6. Columbia University: 4.3 percent.

The Ten States Ranked Best for Business

Based on research done in the early 1980s by the accounting firm Alexander Grant and Company and the Conference of State Manufacturers' Associations.

1. Florida

2. Texas

3. Colorado

4. Kansas

5. North Dakota
6. Mississippi
7. New Mexico
8. Arizona
9. Louisiana
10. Georgia

The Ten States Ranked Worst for Business

Based on research done in the early 1980s by the accounting firm Alexander Grant and Company and the Conference of State Manufacturers' Associations.

1. West Virginia
2. New York
3. Rhode Island
4. Michigan
5. Pennsylvania
6. Illinois
7. Connecticut
8. Massachusetts
9. Maine
10. Kentucky

What the Public Thinks Business Is or Does

1. Adequately develops new products: 84 percent.

2. A good community citizen: 69 percent.

3. Produces safe products: 66 percent.

4. Produces quality products: 64 percent.

5. Pays a fair amount of tax: 42 percent.

6. Controls pollution: 40 percent.

7. Advertises honestly: 37 percent.

8. Makes reasonable profits: 36 percent.

Source: Roper Organization poll, January 1981.

Seven Schools of Economic Thought

1. *Austrian School.*   A group of mostly Austrian economists publishing around the turn of the century who tended to stress the input of the individual rather than the group in economic decisions and direction.

2. *Banking School.*   A group of British economists in the mid-nineteenth century who were extremely nonmonetaristic. They believed that there could never be an excessive amount of money in circulation as long as notes were issued only for loans used to expand production.

3. *Cambridge School.*   A group of Cambridge University economists in the 1930s who were linked to John

Maynard Keynes and, as a result, are also known as post-Keynesians. Unlike the neoclassicists, they tend to focus on the effects of macroeconomic forces, rather than microeconomic ones, on prices.

4. *Chicago School.*   A group of economists associated with the University of Chicago from the 1930s on and including Nobel Prize-winning Milton Friedman. They stress lack of government regulation, market competition, and monetarism.

5. *Classical School.*   A group of early-nineteenth-century British economists that included David Ricardo and John Stuart Mill. These were the economists who drew upon, expanded, and sometimes disagreed with Adam Smith's *The Wealth of Nations*, published in 1776.

6. *Currency School.*   A group of British economists in the mid-nineteenth century who believed the supply of money could be controlled only by 100 percent gold backing. As monetarists, they believed that inflation was due to an oversupply of money.

7. *German Historical School.*   A mid-nineteenth-century group of German economists who disagreed with the classical economists that there were certain economic laws that would operate under all conditions. They emphasized the societal forces that play a part in economics.

Robert Heilbroner and Lester Thurow's Three Greatest Economists

In their book Economics Explained, *noted economists Robert Heilbroner and Lester Thurow list these three men as the world's greatest economists:*

1. Adam Smith (1723–1790), the "patron saint of our discipline." His book *The Wealth of Nations* explained the market process and became the bible of laissez-faire economics.

2. Karl Marx (1818–1883), ". . . perhaps the most remarkable analyst of capitalism's dynamics who ever lived." In his book *Das Kapital*, he pinpointed the problems of capitalism that were inherent risks in a free market.

3. John Maynard Keynes (1883–1946), ". . . the father of the idea of a 'mixed economy' in which the government plays a crucial role." In his book *The General Theory of Employment, Interest and Money*, he pointed out that capitalism sometimes got stuck and was unable to correct problems without intervention.

Adapted from Robert Heilbroner and Lester Thurow, *Economics Explained* (Englewood Cliffs, N.J.: Prentice-Hall, 1982).

Seven Thoughts from Paul Samuelson

Paul Samuelson, Nobel Prize-winning economist and author of Economics, *the best-selling economics text of all time, says:*

1. "Under *laissez faire*, everybody's business is nobody's business. In the good society, everybody's business is everybody's business."

2. "The costs of inflation are what society wants to avoid, not inflation *per se*."

3. "I know that technicians claim to make money by searching for esoteric patterns in market charts. But I

also know that honest men think they can cure cancer with snake oil."

4. "Any broker calling the tune for his customer's investments has a fool for a client."

5. "... the heaven of speculative success is an exclusive club, to which many feel called but for which few are chosen."

6. "Corporations, I am afraid, are persons, born like the rest of us imperfect and subject to sin."

7. "The general laws of technology, despite what you read in the Sunday supplements, are conservative and regular and fairly predictable in their unfoldings."

Eight Important Averages and Indexes

1. *Industrial Production Index.*   A monthly indicator or product output in the manufacturing, mining, and utility industries.

2. *Consumer Price Index.*   A monthly indicator of changes in prices based on what the average urban consumer would pay for food, housing, clothing, transportation, medical expenses, entertainment, and other living expenses.

3. *Producer Price Index.*   A monthly indicator of changes in prices based on the prices received by various industries for their goods.

4. *Dow Jones Averages.*   Four different averages of New York Stock Exchange stocks in various industries. The most quoted is the industrial average, which is used to gauge stock market trends on a daily basis.

5. *Standard & Poor's Indexes.*   Although many different indexes for a variety of industries are published, the most noted is the index of five hundred stocks in the industrial, transportation, utility, and financial fields. It too is released daily.

6. *NYSE Common-Stock Index.*   A half-hourly index of all the common stocks traded on the New York Stock Exchange.

7. *AMEX Index.*   An index of all the common stocks traded on the American Stock Exchange and released daily.

8. *NASDAQ Index.*   An index of over-the-counter stocks traded by members of the National Association of Securities Dealers.

The Twelve Leading Indicators in the Leading Indicator Composite and Their Lead Times

Compiled by the Commerce Department's Bureau of Economic Analysis to predict the state of the economy in upcoming months. Research has shown that these various factors tend to anticipate changes in the economy by an average length in months. For example, on the average, new consumer orders rise six months before the economy picks up and fall six months before the economy takes a downturn.

1. New consumer orders	6.0 months
2. Vendor performance	7.5
3. Inventories	7.8

4.	Plant/equipment orders	8.3
5.	Layoff rate	9.8
6.	Business formation	10.5
7.	Sensitive prices	10.8
8.	Average work week	10.8
9.	Stock market	11.0
10.	Money supply	12.0
11.	Liquid assets	12.3
12.	Housing permits	12.8

Herbert Stein's List of Lessons of the 1960s and 1970s

Herbert Stein, chairman of the President's Council of Economic Advisers during the Nixon administration and noted conservative economist, gives his list of economic truths.

1. "Inflation is a serious problem for the U.S., not something that happens only to banana republics. We can have a high rate of inflation, and once we do it will be difficult to get down."

2. "Achieving price stability does not require a permanently high level of unemployment. That is, there is no permanent trade-off between unemployment and inflation. But the process of getting inflation down will probably require a transitional period of unusually high unemployment."

3. "Getting inflation down and then stabilizing the price level will require first reducing and then stabilizing the rate of growth of the money supply."

4. "Providence has not dictated that the U.S. should have a high rate of economic growth forever, regardless of what we do. If we want high growth, we will have to be careful to follow policies that are conducive to it."

5. "The federal budget contains tens of billions of dollars of expenditures that are nominally addressed to worthy objectives but that are not delivering those objectives, or at least not on a scale that makes the expenditures worthwhile."

6. "Many parts of the federal tax system, especially those that bear most heavily on income from capital, are significantly impeding economic growth."

7. "The constant absorption of a large part of the nation's net saving in financing the federal deficit is a drag on economic growth."

Source: Herbert Stein, "Do We Know What Reagan Economics Is?" *The Wall Street Journal*, March 11, 1982.

Who Benefits from Disinflation

1. Bond holders
2. Debt-free companies
3. Food processors
4. Renters
5. People on fixed incomes
6. Producers of non-price-sensitive goods

7. Companies renegotiating labor contracts

8. Energy users

9. Taxpayers

Who Suffers from Disinflation

1. Debtors

2. Speculators

3. Farmers

4. Landlords

5. Collectors

6. Producers of raw material

7. Companies locked into past labor contracts

8. Energy producers

9. Governments

Thirty Reasons for Declining Productivity

All of the following have been mentioned as possible causes for our declining productivity.

1. *Too Many Workers.* Management prefers using cheap, plentiful but inefficient workers to making costly capital improvements.

2. *Too Many Young Workers.* The baby boom has resulted in a labor market flooded with inexperienced workers.

3. *Undereducated Workers.* The quality of American education is declining, and, consequently, workers are growing less able to use sophisticated machinery.

4. *Overeducated Work Force.* Workers are staying in school longer, becoming overqualified, and getting bored with their jobs.

5. *Labor-Management Conflicts.* Unions and business are cooperating with each other less.

6. *Labor Market Segmentations.* Workers are becoming more specialized and less unified, which demoralizes them and makes them less productive.

7. *Affluence of Work Force.* Workers have enough money so that they don't feel pressured to take high-paying, highly productive jobs.

8. *Changing Values of Work Force.* Workers aren't as interested in career goals as they used to be.

9. *Too Many White-Collar Workers.* There are no adequate standards of productivity in their fields, so they don't work as hard as other workers do.

10. *Fewer People Leaving Low-Productivity Industries.* Fewer people are leaving labor-intensive fields such as agriculture than in the past, so productivity is no longer increasing as dramatically as it once did.

11. *Too Many People in Service Industries.* Productivity is relatively low in retailing, health care, and similar industries. In addition, there are fewer ways to

improve productivity in such jobs than there are in jobs in the manufacturing sector.

12. *Poor Management.*   There are more inexperienced people in decision-making positions than there once were.

13. *Decline in Capital-Labor Ratio.*   There is less investment in capital than there used to be.

14. *Aging Equipment.*   Companies are continuing to use antiquated and inefficient machinery.

15. *Decline in Research and Development.*   Less money is being put into ways of improving productivity than there used to be.

16. *Too Much Technological Change.*   Industries are changing so fast that companies have to constantly pour money into capital improvements.

17. *Too Much Knowledge.*   With the enormous proliferation of technological knowledge, managers and technicians are unable to keep up with developments and so tend to hold fast to outmoded processes.

18. *Too Many Government Regulations.*   Money is being spent on compliance rather than on production.

19. *Too Much Bureaucracy.*   Both governments and organizations are growing more complex and inefficient.

20. *High Taxes.*   They eliminate the incentive to produce more.

21. *Restrictive Monetary Policies.*   It has become too expensive to make long-term investments.

22. *Too Little Savings.*   Not enough money is available for investment.

23. *Too Much Defense Spending*.   Too much of our gross national product is being directed into defense, which is both inefficient and has limited ability to generate wealth.

24. *Too Much Inflation*.   Unstable economic conditions are stifling future investment.

25. *High Energy Prices*.   The cost of producing has gone up drastically as energy prices have skyrocketed.

26. *Declining Natural Resources*.   Productivity will continue to decline as nonrenewable resources are used up.

27. *Family Breakdown*.   So many unhappy homes are producing unhappy and, therefore, unproductive workers.

28. *Crime*.   More money is being spent on security and less on production.

29. *Increased Substance Abuse*.   More and more people are coming to work either drunk or stoned.

30. *Unfavorable Balance of Payments*.   More and more of the products we buy come from other countries.

The Eleven Industries That Showed the Greatest Increase in Productivity from 1975 to 1980

Based on the average annual percentage of change in output per employee per hour. Output equals the dollar value of goods produced divided by labor costs. Where indicated, 1979 figures are used.

1. Wet corn milling   10.6% (1979)

2. Ceramic wall and floor tile   7.5% (1979)

3. Synthetic fibers   6.1%

4. Fluid milk   5.3%

5. Radio and television receiving sets   4.9%

6. Transformers   4.7%

7. Prepared feeds for animals and fowls   4.7% (1979)

8. Malt beverages   4.6%

9. Air transportation   4.6%

10. Household refrigerators and freezers   4.5%

11. Tires and inner tubes   4.5%

Source: *Monthly Labor Review*, May 1982.

The Eleven Industries That Showed the Greatest Decrease in Productivity from 1975 to 1980

Based on the average annual percentage of change in output per employee per hour. Output equals the dollar value of goods produced divided by labor costs. Where indicated, 1979 figures are used.

1. Blended and prepared flour — −5.0% (1979)
2. Brick and structural clay — −3.7%
3. Steel foundries — −2.1%
4. Metal forming-machine tools — −1.8%
5. Eating and drinking places — −1.4%
6. Softwood veneer and plywood — −1.3%
7. Retail food stores — −1.2%
8. Metal household furniture — −0.8% (1979)
9. Gray iron foundries — −0.8%
10. Construction machinery and equipment — −0.6%
11. Paper and plastic products — −0.5% (1979)

Source: *Monthly Labor Review*, May 1982.

Average Annual Inventory Turnover Rates for Various Industries

1. Fast-moving cereal-based foods turn over 64.8 times a year, moderately moving items 13.5 times a year, and slow-moving items 8.8 times a year.

2. Fast-moving chemicals turn over 24.4 times a year, moderately moving items 14.1 times a year, and slow-moving items 7.0 times a year.

3. Fast-moving writing paper turns over 21.9 times a year, moderately moving items 7.0 times a year, and slow-moving items 5.4 times a year.

4. Fast-moving grocery paper turns over 21.3 times a year, moderately moving items 19.3 times a year, and slow-moving items 8.9 times a year.

5. Fast-moving wire and cable tubing turns over 18.5 times a year, moderately moving items 9.8 times a year, and slow-moving items 6.4 times a year.

6. Fast-moving small appliances turn over 5.5 times a year, moderately moving items 4.5 times a year, and slow-moving items 1.6 times a year.

7. Fast-moving automotive window glass turns over 4.7 times a year, moderately moving items 1.7 times a year, and slow-moving items 0.5 times a year.

8. Fast-moving grinding wheels turn over 2.6 times a year, moderately moving items 2.3 times a year, and slow-moving items 0.7 times a year.

9. Fast-moving small appliance parts turn over 1.9 times a year, moderately moving items 1.6 times a year, and slow-moving items 1.4 times a year.

Source: James L. Heskett, Nicholas A. Glaskowsky, Jr., and Robert M. Ivie, *Business Logistics* (New York: Ronald Press, 1973).

Andrew Carnegie on Labor Relations

Andrew Carnegie, noted for his empire-building achievements in the late 1800s, had very definite opinions about workers and his responsibility to them.

1. "The best men as men, and the best workmen, are not walking the streets looking for work. Only the inferior class as a rule is idle."

2. "... capital, labor, and employer [are] a three-legged stool, none before or after the others, all equally indispensable."

3. "... the more I know of working men, the higher I rate their virtues. . . . They have their prejudices and 'red flags,' which have to be respected, for the main root of trouble is ignorance, not hostility."

4. "My experience is that you can always rely upon the great body of working men to do what is right, provided they have not taken up a position and promised their leaders to stand by them. But their loyalty to their leaders, even when mistaken, is something to make us proud of them. Anything can be done with men who have this feeling of loyalty within them. They only need to be treated fairly."

5. "Employers can do so many desirable things for their men at little cost. . . . It pays to go beyond the letter of the bond with your man."

6. "It is for the interest of the employer that his men shall make good earnings and have steady work. . . . High wages are well enough, but they are not to be compared with steady employment."

7. "Labor's hours are to be shortened as we progress. Eight hours will be the rule—eight for work, eight for sleep, and eight for rest and recreation."

8. "It is not capital we need to guard, but helpless labor. If I returned to business tomorrow, fear of labor troubles would not enter my mind, but tenderness for poor and sometimes misguided though well-meaning laborers would fill my heart and soften it; and thereby soften theirs."

9. "The great secret of success in business of all kinds, and especially in manufacturing, where a small saving in each process means a fortune, is a liberal division of profits among the men who help to make them, and the wider the distribution, the better."

The Ten States Where Unionization Is Expected to Increase

Based on the number of union elections per 100,000 employees, and the percentage of those elections unions win.

1. Alaska

2. Hawaii

3. Washington

4. Oregon

5. Michigan

6. California

7. Colorado

8. Maine

9. Iowa

10. Ohio

Source: John G. Kilgour, *Preventive Labor Relations* (New York: AMACOM, 1981). Data was taken from 41 NLRB Annual Report 244 (Table 15A), 1976.

The Ten States Least Likely to See Increased Unionization

Based on the number of union elections per 100,000 employees, and the percentage of those elections unions win.

1. Virginia

2. North Carolina

3. Utah

4. South Carolina

5. Florida

6. Vermont

7. Idaho

8. Maryland

9. Delaware

10. Texas

Source: John G. Kilgour, *Preventive Labor Relations* (New York: AMACOM, 1981). Data was taken from 41 NLRB Annual Report 244 (Table 15A), 1976.

Eleven Events That May Trigger a Unionizing Drive

1. *A Change in Ownership.* If employees are apprehensive about the new owners, they may be interested in unionizing to protect whatever concessions they won from the previous owners.

2. *A Change in Management.*   Just as new owners can trigger employee apprehension, so can new managers. Actions that were tolerated from the old managers because employees were familiar with them may not be tolerated from strangers.

3. *A Change in Policy.*   Any sudden or unexpected change on the part of top management will lead employees to think communication lines are closed to them. On the assumption that management isn't looking out for their interests, they may turn to unions.

4. *Nepotism.*   Putting a relative in charge—one whom employees don't know well—may increase their suspicions about management's motives.

5. *Layoff of Employees.*   If employees assume that their jobs are in jeopardy or that their incomes will be going down, they may turn to unions for protection.

6. *An Unpopular Firing.*   If an employee is dismissed without good explanation, employees may turn to unions to serve as arbitrators in the future.

7. *A Breach in Seniority.*   If benefits and penalties are not accorded on the basis of seniority—an evaluative technique generally acceptable to most employees—they may turn to unions for enforcement.

8. *Unsafe Conditions.*   If employees consider their work area to be hazardous and feel that management has no interest in correcting the situation, they may feel unions are their only recourse.

9. *Arbitrary Wage and Benefit Scales.*   If employees feel compensation is rewarded inequitably, they may wish to have changes imposed from the outside.

10. *Sexual Harassment.*   While not all employees may be sympathetic to the plight of women in the workplace, an incident can be a rallying point.

11. *An Economic Downturn.*   Financial pressures on the company may alter working conditions and lead employees to seek a way to respond with their own pressure.

Thirty-seven Business Handbooks

Complete guides to whatever you need to know in the field.

1. *Business Management Handbook*, by Jacob Kay Lasser. Edited by Bernard Greisman. New York: McGraw-Hill, 1968.

2. *Handbook of Business Administration*, edited by Harold Bright Maynard. New York: McGraw-Hill, 1967.

3. *Office Management Handbook*, edited by Harry L. Wylie. New York: Ronald, 1958.

4. *The Dartnell Office Administration*, edited by Robert S. Minor and Clark W. Petridge. Chicago: Dartnell, 1975.

5. *Business Executive's Handbook*, by Stanley M. Brown and Lillian Doris. New York: Prentice-Hall, 1953.

6. *The Chief Executive's Handbook*, edited by John Desmond Glover and Gerald A. Simon. Homewood, Ill.: Dow Jones-Irwin, 1976.

7. *Treasurer's Handbook*, by J. Fred Weston and Maurice B. Goudzwaard. Homewood, Ill.: Dow Jones-Irwin, 1976.

8. *Financial Handbook*, edited by Edward I. Altman. New York: Ronald, 1981.

9. *Financial Executive's Handbook*, by Richard F. Vancil. Homewood, Ill.: Dow Jones-Irwin, 1980.

10. *Handbook of Modern Accounting*, edited by Sidney Davidson. New York: McGraw-Hill, 1970.

11. *Accountant's Handbook*, edited by Rufus Wilson, Walter G. Kell, and Norton M. Bedford. New York: Ronald, 1970.

12. *Accountant's Desk Handbook*, by Albert P. Ameiss and Nicholas A. Kargas. Englewood Cliffs, N.J.: Prentice-Hall, 1977.

13. *The Managerial and Cost Accountant's Handbook*, by Homer A. Black and James D. Edwards. Homewood, Ill.: Dow Jones-Irwin, 1979.

14. *Handbook for Auditors*, edited by James A. Cashin. New York: McGraw-Hill, 1971.

15. *Marketing Handbook*, by Albert Wesley Frey and Gerald Albaum. New York: Ronald, 1965.

16. *Handbook of Modern Marketing*, edited by Victor P. Buell and Carl Heyel. New York: McGraw-Hill, 1970.

17. *The Dartnell Marketing Manager's Handbook*, by Steuart Henderson Britt. Chicago: Dartnell, 1973.

18. *Handbook of Marketing Research*, by Robert Ferber. New York: McGraw-Hill, 1974.

19. *The Dartnell Sales Manager's Handbook*, edited by Ovid Riso. Chicago: Dartnell, 1968.

20. *The Dartnell Sales Promotion Handbook*, edited by Ovid Riso. Chicago: Dartnell, 1966.

21. *The Dartnell Advertising Manager's Handbook*, by Richard H. Stansfield. Chicago: Dartnell, 1969.

22. *Handbook of Advertising Management*, edited by Roger Barton. New York: McGraw-Hill, 1970.

23. *Direct Mail and Mail Order Handbook*, by Richard S. Hodgson. Chicago: Dartnell, 1980.

24. *Printing and Promotion Handbook: How to Plan, Produce, and Use Printing, Advertising, and Direct Mail*, by Daniel Melcher and Nancy Larrick. New York: McGraw-Hill, 1966.

25. *The Dartnell Public Relations Handbook*, by Richard W. Darrow, Dan J. Forrestal, and Aubrey O. Cookman. Chicago: Dartnell, 1967.

26. *Lesly's Public Relations Handbook*, by Philip Lesly. Englewood Cliffs, N.J.: Prentice-Hall, 1971.

27. *The Dartnell Personnel Director's Handbook*, edited by J. C. Aspley. Chicago: Dartnell, 1969.

28. *Handbook of Personnel Management and Labor Relations*, by Dale Yoder and others. New York: McGraw-Hill, 1958.

29. *Handbook of Modern Personnel Administration*, by Joseph J. Famularo. New York: McGraw-Hill, 1972.

30. *Training and Development Handbook: A Guide to Human Resource Development*, by Robert L. Craig. New York: McGraw-Hill, 1976.

31. *Production Handbook*, by Jules Irwin and others. New York: Ronald, 1972.

32. *Purchasing Handbook: Standard Reference Book on Policies, Practices, and Procedures Utilized in Departments Responsible for Purchasing Management or Materials Management*, edited by George W. Aljian. New York: McGraw-Hill, 1973.

33. *The Bankers' Handbook*, by William Hubert Baughn and Charles E. Walker. Homewood, Ill.: Dow Jones-Irwin, 1978.

34. *Financial Analyst's Handbook*, by Sumner N. Levine. Homewood, Ill.: Dow Jones-Irwin, 1975.

35. *Stock Market Handbook: Reference Manual for the Securities Industry*, by Frank G. Zarb and Gabriel T. Kerekes. Homewood, Ill.: Dow Jones-Irwin, 1983.

36. *The McGraw-Hill Construction Business Handbook: A Practical Guide to Accounting, Credit, Finance, Insurance, and Law for the Construction Industry*, edited by Robert F. Cushman. New York: McGraw-Hill, 1978.

37. *Life and Health Insurance Handbook*, by Davis Weinert Gregg and Vane B. Lucas. Homewood, Ill.: Richard D. Irwin, 1973.

2

THE BUSINESS
WORLD

Ways and Means from
Mom-and-Pop Shops
to Corporate Boardrooms

The McKinsey 7-S Framework

McKinsey consultants Thomas J. Peters and Robert H. Waterman, Jr. (authors of In Search of Excellence*), along with McKinsey colleagues Julien R. Phillips and James Bennett, and Professors Richard Tanner Pascale and Anthony G. Athos (authors of* The Art of Japanese Management*), have developed a seven-factor framework of use in diagnosing problems in organizational effectiveness and designing improvements:*

1. *Superordinate goal(s).* In what way(s) does the organization intend to be distinctive? What key shared values define criteria for success and "the way we do things around here"?

2. *Strategy.* In what businesses and markets does the company plan to compete? What sustainable competitive advantage(s) will it seek?

3. *Skills.* What activities, important to its success, is the company distinctively good at? Poor at?

4. *Structure.* How is authority and accountability for major decisions and tasks assigned? What relationships of power and influence exist?

5. *Staff.* What are the outstanding "demographic" characteristics of dominant employee groups in the com-

pany, e.g., academic training, main business or departments worked in, distinctive accomplishments?

6. *Systems*. What are the routine managerial processes through which problems get identified, decisions made and executed?

7. *Style*. What are the characteristic patterns of behavior of senior managers in the company, e.g., allocation of time and attention?

Source: Thomas J. Peters, Robert H. Waterman, Jr., and Julien R. Phillips, "Structure Is Not Organization," *Business Horizons*, June 1980.

The Five Basic Parts of an Organization

Henry Mintzberg, professor of management at McGill University, breaks the corporation down into five parts.

1. *The Operating Core*. Those people responsible for production—those whose work involves gathering the raw material (or parts or information), processing it into finished goods and services, and distributing them or supporting those who do.

2. *The Strategic Apex*. Those who supervise, who represent the company to outsiders, and who plan.

3. *The Middle Line*. Those who supervise the people below them and report to the people above them.

4. *The Technostructure*. The analysts who "exist to standardize the work of others."

5. *The Support Staff.*   Those who are maintained to pro- vide the company with more control over the adjunct goods and services it uses.

Source: Henry Mintzberg. *The Structuring of Organizations* (Englewood Cliffs, N.J.: Prentice-Hall, 1979).

Six Ways to Group Organizational Activities

According to Henry Mintzberg, organizational activities are usually grouped in one of the following ways:

1. *By Knowledge and Skill.*   Either by department (as in a college—history, sociology, psychology) or by level (such as trainee, assistant, and manager).

2. *By Work Process and Function.*   "Perhaps the most common example of this is grouping by 'business function'—manufacturing, marketing, engineering, finance, and so on, some of these groups being line and others staff."

3. *By Time.*   Grouped by shift.

4. *By Output.*   Grouped by product (such as small- appliances, large-appliances, industrial-equipment, and military-hardware divisions) or by service (such as advertising, public relations, and personal-image con- sulting).

5. *By Client.*   Based on to whom the product or service is being sold, marketed, or addressed (such as trade books, el-hi books, college texts, technical books).

6. *By Place.*   Geographic location on whatever scale, whether it be international (such as Europe, Asia, North America), within a factory (such as west wing, east

wing), or on a body (such as cardiology, ob-gyn, opthalmology).

Source: Henry Mintzberg, *The Structuring of Organizations* (Englewood Cliffs, N.J.: Prentice-Hall, 1979.)

What Happens as a Company Grows

1. The CEO becomes less an entrepreneur and more a team leader and conflict resolver.

2. Fewer decisions are made at the top.

3. Workers have less contact with top managers and more with middle managers.

4. Titles become more important, and jobs become more defined.

5. Communication becomes more standardized and more formal.

6. More rules and policies are established and written down.

7. Staff is expanded and given more authority.

8. Employee evaluations become more standardized and statistically analyzed.

9. Operations become more complex.

10. More money is available for the hiring of experts.

Adapted from George Strauss, "Adolescence in Organization Growth: Problems, Pains, Possibilities," *Organization Dynamics*, Spring 1974.

Lockheed's Span-of-Control Variables

Lockheed has determined that the optimal span of control must be adjusted to accommodate the following:

1. *Functional Similarity.*   The more similar the functions are, the broader the span of control.

2. *Geographical Closeness.*   The more concentrated the work area is, the broader the span of control.

3. *Functional Complexity.*   The more complex the functions are, the narrower the span of control.

4. *Need for Direction.*   The more the subordinates need supervision, the narrower the span of control.

5. *Need for Coordination.*   The greater the need for coordination is, the narrower the span of control.

6. *Planning Demands.*   The more involved the plan is, the narrower the span of control.

7. *Managerial Help.*   The more help the superior receives, the broader the span of control.

Source: Joe Kelly, *How Managers Manage* (Englewood Cliffs, N.J.: Prentice-Hall, 1980).

The Five Steps in Learning to Love Corporations

In his article "Learning to Love the Modern Corporation," James L. Cullather offers the following bits of advice for those sixties leftovers and ivory-tower types who want to embrace capitalism but can't yet accept the worth of corporations.

1. Recite little sayings about corporations by substituting the word "corporation" for "man" in any familiar expression of trust, friendship, goodwill, or charity— e.g., "I never met a corporation I didn't like."

2. Think of corporations in human terms: as flawed individuals who might have had "unhappy beginnings" or unloving parents.

3. Look at annual report covers, which will help to remind you of all the wonderful things corporations do.

4. Look for signs that corporations care—rehabilitation programs, products for the handicapped, sponsorship of educational television programs.

5. Read the social-responsibility reports in which corporations outline their charitable contributions, their affirmative-action programs, and their efforts to preserve the environment. Sometimes they will even tell you what they haven't done yet, like hire enough women.

Source: James L. Cullather, "Learning to Love the Modern Corporation," *Business and Society Review*, Summer 1982.

Six Ways to Implement Corporate Change

1. *Education.* People will be less resistant if you tell them as much as you possibly can about the change beforehand.

2. *Participation.* People are often less resistant to change when they are asked to help plan it and make it.

3. *Facilitation.* People sometimes need help while making a change. They may need support and a chance to express their apprehension.

4. *Negotiation.* If people feel a change is not in their best interests, they may be willing to cooperate only if they get something they want in exchange.

5. *Manipulation.* Sometimes people can be led through a change without realizing it until after the fact. This technique works if the change will definitely be in their interests and they realize this once they've made it.

6. *Coercion.* Forced change is desirable only when management has no other alternative—when change must take place because without it the organization will cease to function.

Source: John P. Kotter and Leonard A. Schlesinger, "Choosing Strategies for Change," *Harvard Business Review*, March–April 1979.

Six Models of Social Responsibility

1. *The Austere Model.* Only the stockholders' financial concerns are considered.

2. *The Investment Model.* The long-term needs of the firm are considered. This would include programs that promote a healthy business climate and positive attitudes toward business.

3. *The Household Model.* The employees' needs are considered and take priority over all else.

4. *The Vendor Model.* The consumers' needs are primary. This would include programs that encourage consumer protection, fair pricing, and development of products that consumers most want.

5. *The Civic Model.* The needs of the community take priority. Political and social programs are encouraged.

6. *The Artistic Model.* Creativity is valued above all. This would include arts endowments and working conditions that encourage imagination and innovation.

Source: Clarence C. Walton, *Corporate Social Responsibilities* (Boston: Kent Publishing Company, 1967).

Corporate Social Responsibilities That Take Time and Money

How 248 companies responded when asked which activities involve significant commitments of resources.

1. Minority employment and advancement: 98 percent.

2. Educational programs and sponsorship: 96 percent.

3. Minority recruitment: 80 percent.

4. Career-opportunity programs: 77 percent.

5. Pollution-control equipment: 76 percent.

6. Productivity improvement: 73 percent.

7. Contributions to the arts: 71 percent.

8. Minority training programs: 71 percent.

9. Management-improvement programs: 70 percent.

10. Environmentally compatible plant designs: 68 percent.

Source: John J. Corson and George Steiner, *Measuring Business's Social Performance: The Corporate Social Audit* (New York: Committee for Economic Development, 1974).

What Men Think of Affirmative Action

Based on a national survey of 884 men in a variety of nonprofit and for-profit organizations. The majority have been to college and hold managerial or supervisory positions.

1. 50 percent agree that women have greater promotion opportunities than men.

2. 45 percent agree that some jobs should stay men's jobs and some should stay women's.

3. 27 percent agree that women's liberation scares management.

4. 26 percent agree that women belong at home.

5. 26 percent agree that laws force organizations to favor women.

6. 23 percent agree that there is more emphasis on training of women than on training of men.

7. 21 percent agree that "men should always be the backbone of the organization."

8. 19 percent agree that "women can get complaints resolved more easily than men."

9. 17 percent agree that disaster will result if women get too much power.

10. 14 percent "resent women's attempts to get more power."

11. 13 percent agree that women get too many breaks.

12. 10 percent agree that women get more opportunities for development than men.

13. 5 percent agree that "women have too much say on politics and decisions."

Source: Benson Rosen and Thomas H. Jerdee, "Coping with Affirmative Action Backlash," *Business Horizons*, August 1979.

Eleven Reasons Corporations Should Support the Arts

1. *Public Relations*.   Sponsorship of an arts program can generate public awareness of your company, just as a sponsorship of a show on educational television will.

2. *Image Enhancement.*   Just as Hallmark uses its televised cultural specials to convey an image, you can link program sponsorship or arts commissions and purchases to your company's position in the community.

3. *Image Focus.*   By using your funds selectively, you can concentrate on areas that convey your company's special interests or strengths—e.g., developing a collection of pieces by artists in your region to emphasize your geographical roots.

4. *Employee Benefits.*   Art works enhance the working atmosphere.

5. *Inspiration.*   Art and cultural events promote creativity among employees.

6. *Sales Improvement.*   You can commission new artwork or purchase copies of already created work and perhaps incorporate such items into your product line.

7. *Consumer Motivation.*   By holding cultural events at your place of business, you can attract consumers who might otherwise not stop by.

8. *Community Involvement.*   By involving employees in cultural activities, your company can make valuable contacts.

9. *Client Acquisition.*   By working with arts groups, you may be able to pick up business from wealthy artists and their patrons.

10. *Client Relations.*   You can treat special customers to free theater tickets, choice seats at special events, and parties amid your art collection.

11. *Tax Deductions.*   You can contribute goods to nonprofit arts groups and write them off.

Six Reasons Businessmen
Act Unethically

Based on a survey of 1,227 Harvard Business Review readers and listed in order of rank.

1. For personal financial reasons.

2. As a result of society's values.

3. Because of influence by peers.

4. As a result of the industry's values.

5. As a result of their companies' stated or unstated values.

6. Because of influence by superiors.

Source: Steven N. Brenner and Carl A. Molander, "Is the Ethics of Business Changing?" *Harvard Business Review*, January–February 1977.

Six Factors That Raise
Ethical Standards

Based on a survey of 1,227 Harvard Business Review readers.

1. Publicity and media scrutiny: 31 percent.

2. Feedback from the public and higher societal standards: 20 percent.

3. Government involvement: 10 percent.

4. Improved managerial education: 9 percent.

5. New definitions of business responsibility as defined by a younger electorate and consumer activists: 5 percent.

6. Management's growing interest in social responsibility: 5 percent.

Source: Steven N. Brenner and Carl A. Molander, "Is the Ethics of Business Changing?" *Harvard Business Review*, January–February 1977.

The Fifteen Unhealthiest Industries

Based on the total number of reported cases of injury and illness per 100 workers.

1. Lumber and wood products

2. Food

3. Fabricated metal products

4. Anthracite mining

5. Furniture and fixtures

6. Primary metal

7. Rubber and plastics products

8. Stone, clay, and glass products

9. Heavy construction

10. General building

11. Special trade construction

12. Trucking and warehousing

13. Machinery other than electrical

14. Water transportation

15. Air transportation

Ten Tactics to Use When the Safety of Your Product Is Questioned

1. Pull all regular advertising. It may be inappropriate and possibly embarrassing at this time.

2. Stop production at least temporarily and publicize this.

3. Announce a voluntary recall if a pattern of deaths or serious injury seems to be linked to your product.

4. Publicly express concern over the problem, but don't defend, explain, or apologize for your product.

5. Publicly throw your support behind efforts to alleviate the problem (e.g., offer reward money to track down terrorists sabotaging your product, set up research programs to investigate links between your product—and similar ones—and diseases, etc).

6. Set up a hot line to be called by consumers with questions, tips, concerns, etc.

7. Announce a campaign to develop new, problem-free products that will lead the way in the future (be the first with tamper-proof containers, crash-resistant automobiles, child-proof toys, etc.).

8. Offer incentives to encourage consumers to try your new, improved product (coupons, rebates, etc.).

9. Offer incentives to retailers to restock your product (discounts, cooperative advertising, etc.).

10. Act quickly to regain consumer loyalty.

3

POSITIONS

**What's in a Title and Other Important
Things About Image**

Ten Management Roles

Henry Mintzberg, professor of management at McGill University, has analyzed what managers do all day, and lists the following activities.

Interpersonal Roles

1. *Figurehead.* The ceremonial duties: greeting VIPs, sending out birthday cards to employees, cutting ribbons, and so on. Twelve percent of all time spent in contact with other people and 17 percent of all the mail coming in are related to status.

2. *Leader.* The most talked-about role: directing subordinates.

3. *Liaison.* Dealing with people "outside [the] vertical chain of command." Forty-four percent of all time spent dealing with others involves outsiders, compared with 48 percent dealing with subordinates and only 7 percent with superiors.

Informational Roles

4. *Monitor.* The gathering of information: reading newspapers and research reports, asking questions of subordinates, picking up bits and pieces from a net-

work of contacts. "A good part of the information a manager collects in his monitor role arrives in verbal form, often as gossip, hearsay, and speculation."

5. *Disseminator*. Passing on to subordinates information that they need.

6. *Spokesman*. Sending information to people outside the unit.

Decisional Roles

7. *Entrepreneur*. Implementing new ideas: starting projects within the unit.

8. *Disturbance Handler*. Reaction to unexpected situations. "Disturbances arise not only because poor managers ignore situations until they reach crisis proportions, but also because good managers cannot possibly anticipate all the consequences of the actions they take."

9. *Resource Allocator*. Deciding "who will get what in [the] organizational unit," including the manager's time.

10. *Negotiator*. "Studies of managerial work at all levels indicate that managers spend considerable time in negotiations...."

Mintzberg notes that sales managers "seem to spend relatively more of their time in the interpersonal roles... production managers give relatively more attention to the decisional roles... staff managers spend the most time in the informational roles...."

Source: Henry Mintzberg, "The Manager's Job: Folklore and Fact," *Harvard Business Review*, July–August 1975.

Ten Management Styles

In his book Managing with Style and Making It Work for You, *Henry O. Golightly, founder of Golightly and Company International, a consulting firm, lists the following:*

1. *Management by Inaction.* The manager who does nothing, or at least puts off doing anything. He may be too fearful, uncertain, or bored to take action, but he also assumes that "if you ignore a problem, it will go away, or at least get better." He functions best in areas where change comes slowly and where he works for people who prefer to make their own decisions rather than to delegate them.

2. *Management by Detail.* The manager who researches a problem to death instead of solving it. He works best with people who appreciate his information, don't depend on him for quick or dramatic decisions, and will set deadlines for him.

3. *Management by Invisibility.* The manager who makes himself inaccessible for various reasons, thus forcing subordinates to do more of the work and take the heat. He works best with people who don't need to interact with him, but he needs the presence of a few people so he isn't allowed to isolate himself totally.

4. *Management by Consensus.* The manager who wants decisions to be a group effort. He either wants harmony or is afraid to make decisions by himself. He does not work well with people who won't interact with him or who expect him to generate his own ideas. But he does work well in decentralized companies that stress human relations.

5. *Management by Manipulation.* The manager who is most concerned with getting people to do what he wants. He values control for control's sake. He works well with people who are not likely to challenge his

methods and may even use them for their benefit. He works best in situations with well-defined goals for which he can aim.

6. *Management by Rejection.* The manager who is overwhelmingly negative. He picks apart all ideas and resists change. He can make a contribution by tempering hastily thought-out or ill-advised schemes conceived by more dynamic co-workers.

7. *Management by Survival.* The manager who looks out primarily for himself. He has a subordinate mentality—a good follower but one unwilling to take risks. He works best "in an organization large and stable enough to value the consistent performer who is not a 'tiger.'"

8. *Management by Despotism.* The manager who rules with an iron fist and expects complete subjugation. He works best under people who leave him alone to run things and will get cooperation from subordinates by paying them well.

9. *Management by Creativity.* The manager who manages instinctively. He bases his actions and decisions on hunches, which may or may not be right. He works best with people who will respect his ideas, if not always follow them, who will leave him alone to be creative, or who will organize and implement his good ideas and pass over his bad ones.

10. *Management by Leadership.* The manager who listens to his subordinates and then shows them direction. He values both interaction and goals. He adopts techniques from all the other management styles and knows when to use them and how to keep them in balance.

Adapted from Henry O. Golightly, *Managing with Style and Making It Work for You* (New York: AMACOM, 1977).

Ten Types of Management

1. *Management by Objectives* (MBO). The organization sets overall objectives, and then all managers set personal objectives. It helps to get everyone thinking in a set time frame but can be slow to respond to new developments.

2. *Management by Exception* (MBE). Managers delegate as much responsibility and activity as possible to those below them and step in only when problems or unusual situations arise. It helps managers focus on critical areas but requires excellent feedback.

3. *Management by Decision Models* (MBDM). Decisions are based on projections generated by artificially constructed situations. It helps management see the possible consequences of their actions but tends to be overly simplistic.

4. *Management by Styles* (MBS). Managers adjust their approaches to meet situational needs. It is flexible but demands more skill than some managers possess.

5. *Management by Competitive Edge* (MBCE). Individuals and groups within the organization compete against one another to see which can achieve the best results. It helps the skillful people rise to the top but can undermine cooperative efforts.

6. *Management by Coaching and Development* (MBCD). Managers see themselves primarily as employee trainers. It helps to bring out the best in everyone, but many managers are not good teachers.

7. *Management by Information Systems* (MBIS). Managers depend on data generated within the company to help them increase efficiency and interrelatedness. It helps management to see the organization as a whole but takes time and money.

8. *Management by Matrices* (MBM).   Managers study charted variables to discern their interrelatedness, probable cause and effect, and available options. It helps managers put organizational variables into perspective but can oversimplify those relationships.

9. *Management by Work Simplification* (MBWS). Managers constantly seek ways to simplify processes and reduce expenses. It helps management keep red tape to a minimum but may meet employee resistance.

10. *Management by Organizational Development* (MBOD).   Managers constantly seek to improve employee relations and communication. It helps managers to focus on employees but may net few short-term changes.

Adapted from Paul Mali, "The Practice of Modern Management," in *Management Handbook* (New York: John Wiley & Sons, 1981).

Seventeen Factors That Make a Job Powerful

1. Has few rules to follow.

2. Held by few predecessors.

3. Has few set routines.

4. Offers variety.

5. Doesn't encourage predictability.

6. Encourages innovation.

7. Allows flexibility.

8. Allows decision making.

9. Is centrally located.

10. Offers visibility.

11. Is relevant to current corporate concerns.

12. Contains broad scope.

13. Includes frequent personal interaction.

14. Allows access to top management.

15. Requires group presentations.

16. Allows problem-solving input.

17. Includes supervision of fast-trackers.

Adapted from Rosabeth Moss Kanter, "Power Failures in Management Circuits," *Harvard Business Review*, July–August 1979.

Ten Characteristics
of Entrepreneurs

In several studies on motivation and achievement, the following entrepreneurial personality characteristics have been delineated:

1. *High Achievement Needs.*   The desire to meet challenging goals.

2. *Moderate Risk-taking.*   The ability to assess situations and the good sense to try only those that have a reasonable possibility for success.

3. *Expectation of Success.*   The assumption that most attempted endeavors will pay off.

4. *Self-confidence.*   Trust in one's skills.

5. *High Energy Level.*   The ability to accomplish a great deal in a limited amount of time.

6. *Desire for Feedback.*   The ability to utilize information, positive or negative, to assess progress.

7. *Belief in Compensation.*   Financial reward is valued as proof of competence.

8. *Future Orientation.*   An inclination toward planning.

9. *Organizational Ability.*   Can focus on goals and work with people and plans.

10. *Responsibility Needs.*   A strong desire to feel personally accountable for actions, successes, and failures.

Seven Managerial Qualities and How They Are Assessed

Some companies routinely test new managers to identify their strengths and assess their managerial potential. Tests are used to predict the following skills:

1. *Administrative Skills.* The in-basket test. You are given a random pile of memos, notes, letters, and other written material, given some background on an imaginary company, and told to make decisions about priorities, delegation, investigation, and planning within an allotted period of time.

2. *Interpersonal Skills.* Group activities such as business games and leaderless discussions.

3. *Intellectual Ability.* Paper-and-pencil tests.

4. *Emotional Stability.* Group activities and the in-basket test.

5. *Work Motivation.* Projective personality tests and work situation simulations.

6. *Career Orientation.* Projective personality tests, interview reports, and personality questionnaires.

7. *Dependency on Others.* Projective personality tests.

Source: Douglas W. Bray, Donald L. Grant, and Richard J. Campbell, "Studying Careers and Assessing Ability," in *The Failure of Success*, ed. Alfred J. Marrow (New York: AMACOM, 1972).

Nine Complaints from Top Management About Marketing People

1. Marketing people don't seem to focus on what top management is saying.

2. They keep using the same old ideas.

3. They can't seem to read or predict the market.

4. They are too cautious.

5. They want too much mobility.

6. They don't get enough out of their budgets.

7. They look at the wrong numbers—sales rather than profits.

8. They don't have a good system for performance evaluation.

9. They have been promising too much of the wrong thing to consumers.

Source: Bill Abrams, "Top Executives View Marketers as Myopic and Unimaginative," *The Wall Street Journal*, October 9, 1980.

Seven Kinds of Salesmen

1. *Route-Server*. One who makes deliveries along a specific route and takes orders in the process.

2. *Order-Taker*. One who remains at a sales outlet and waits for customers to come to him.

3. *Jobber*. One who stocks outlets in a variety of locations and takes orders as supplies run down.

4. *Missionary.* One who does not transact business but merely stays in touch with customers to promote good-will.

5. *Technician.* One who shows the customer how to use the product and helps to install it.

6. *Motivator.* One who first creates the need and then sells the product.

7. *Service-Seller.* One who sells intangibles rather than products.

Adapted from Robert N. McMurry, "The Mystique of Super-Salesmanship," *Harvard Business Review*, March–April 1961.

What an Executive Assistant Needs to Have

1. The ability to travel well, sometimes at the drop of a hat.

2. An eye for details, so he can handle what his boss doesn't want to be bothered with.

3. Loyalty to the firm, willingness to sacrifice personal glory for a greater good.

4. Admiration for his boss.

5. Communication skills, so he can speak for his boss if necessary.

6. A pleasant personality, so he can get along with anyone he has to deal with.

Adapted from Walter Kiechel III, "The Executive Assistant," *Fortune*, November 15, 1982.

Seven Things That Internal Consultants Do

Rather than contracting for management consulting services only when they are needed, some companies employ full-time consultants who do the following:

1. Straighten out bottlenecks.

2. Anticipate and head off bottlenecks.

3. Keep management abreast of the latest management techniques.

4. Prepare reports and make recommendations.

5. Follow through on recommendations by implementing programs.

6. Observe and counsel top management.

7. Work with external consultants.

Adapted from Robert E. Kelly, "Should You Have an Internal Consultant?" *Harvard Business Review*, November–December 1979.

Eight Reasons to Use Management Consultants

1. *To Limit Staff.*   It is often more cost-effective to farm out special projects when they come up than to have underutilized employees on hand when it's business as usual.

2. *Expertise.*   Occasionally problems develop that are beyond the capabilities of your current staff.

3. *Broad Experience.*   Having worked with many different companies, consultants are often in a position to know more strategies than you do.

4. *New Insights.*   By staying current on the latest research and specializing in problem solving, consultants can often suggest ideas that you have never thought of.

5. *Objectivity.*   Managers are not always able to divorce their decisions from their personal feelings and goals; consultants are not so likely to have conflicts of interest.

6. *Lack of Politics.*   Sometimes consultants can suggest and implement changes that in-house managers are unable to do because of ongoing power struggles.

7. *Discreetness.*   Because they are often unknown to most of the company's employees, consultants can gather information unavailable to in-house staff. In addition, they can often represent corporate clients anonymously when dealing with other companies.

8. *Wide Range of Sources.*   Consultants have access to a network of contacts different from that of most corporate executives.

Six Professional Pitfalls

1. *"The Special Language Pitfall."*   Accustomed to using jargon among themselves, professionals sometimes forget that this language is often unintelligible to co-workers and clients. As a result, communication breaks down between professionals and those they are supposed to serve.

2. *"The Professional Polish Pitfall."*   Professionals take pride in their work and often aim for perfection. But such efforts can hamper results if they take precedence over problem solving.

3. *"The Unnecessary Services Pitfall."*   A desire to try out the latest techniques or to display all their expertise can lead professionals to engage in overkill—offering more to clients and management than they need or can even use and benefit from.

4. *"The Professional Blinders Pitfall."*   Not surprisingly, specialists specialize. They take large problems and narrow them down until they fit into their areas of expertise. Unfortunately, this often distorts problem-solving efforts.

5. *"The Status, Access, Mobility Pitfall."*   Professionals in staff positions in an organization often have access to top management. This can, however, hurt their credibility with the rank and file. Therefore, professionals must be mindful of their perceived status when approaching other employees.

6. *"The Birds-of-a-Feather Pitfall."*   Because they share similar backgrounds and interests, professionals sometimes seek out each other rather than spend time with their nonprofessional co-workers. This can make them seem aloof and unfriendly.

Source: Joseph A. Litterer, "Pitfalls for 'Professionals,'" *Personnel Journal*, May 1982.

Eighteen Thoughts from Peter Drucker

Peter Drucker has been called a "business philosopher" and is perhaps the most widely respected management theorist alive today. He has been quoted as saying:

1. "Until perhaps as late as twenty years ago, 'female emancipation' largely meant freeing women from the necessity of taking a paying job."

2. "Nothing discourages people as much as managerial incompetence."

3. "In terms of the human resource, the computer is a monstrosity; it expects people to do totally routinized, moron's work and exercise judgment and imagination in doing it."

4. "...the computer is over-engineered, and as long as you have the human factor in the input, you're going to get mistakes."

5. "Innovative ideas are like frogs' eggs; of a thousand hatched, only one or two survive to maturity."

6. "One never hears talk of 'creativity' in innovative companies—'creativity' is the buzzword of those who don't innovate."

7. "...every time the staff takes on a new task, it should abandon an old one."

8. "Don't ever put anyone into a staff job...unless he or she has successfully held a number of operating jobs, preferably in more than one functional area."

9. "Unless challenged, every organization tends to become slack, easygoing, diffuse."

10. "Many of the giants of tomorrow will be companies that either do not exist today or are so small as to be almost invisible."

11. "Management by objectives works if you know the objectives. Ninety percent of the time you don't."

12. "If a client leaves this room feeling he has learned a lot he hadn't known before, he is either a stupid client or I've done a poor job. He should leave saying, I know all this—why haven't I done anything about it?"

13. "Don't put the fate of your business in the delusions of economists."

14. "Long-range planning does not deal with future decisions, but with the futurity of present decisions."

15. "Strong people always have strong weaknesses."

16. "Fast personnel decisions are likely to be wrong."

17. "Success in running a business carries by itself no promise of success outside business."

18. "If a manager spends more than 10 percent of his time on 'human relations' the group is probably too large."

Socrates' Rules for Managers

According to his disciple Xenophon (author of Memorabilia *about the life and teachings of Socrates) Socrates said this about managers:*

1. They should "render those under their command obedient and submissive."

2. They should "appoint fitting persons to fulfill various duties."

3. They should "punish the bad, and . . . honor the good."

4. They should "render those under them well disposed toward them."

5. They should "gain for themselves allies and auxiliaries."

6. They should "be careful of their resources."

7. They should "be attentive and industrious in their respective duties."

8. They should "gain superiority over [their] enemies."

Nineteen Suggestions for Managers from Confucius

1. "The perfect gentleman demands it of himself; the mean man, of others."

2. "The perfect gentleman reaches complete understanding of the main issues; the mean man reaches complete understanding of the petty details."

3. "The perfect man does not accept a man for his words alone; he does not reject a suggestion because of the man alone."

4. "The perfect gentleman, out of a sense of pride, does not engage in strifes; out of consideration for the group as a whole he does not join cliques."

5. "The perfect gentleman gives his approval not to techniques but to the capacity for great responsibility. The mean man does just the opposite."

6. "The perfect gentleman is sparing in words but prodigal in deeds."

7. "The perfect gentleman does not work a people until he has won their confidence, otherwise they will feel

that he is being severe with them. He does not remonstrate with a superior until he has won his confidence, otherwise he will feel that he is being maligned."

8. "The faults of the perfect gentleman may be compared to eclipses of the sun and moon. While they are being committed everybody sees them, but once he changes everybody gazes up at him in respect."

9. "It is indeed harmful to come under the sway of utterly new and strange doctrines."

10. "He who engages solely in interested action will make himself many enemies."

11. "If everybody dislikes it, it must be looked into. If everybody likes it, it must be looked into."

12. "Clever talk and domineering manner have little to do with being man at his best."

13. "Do not worry about not holding high position; worry rather about playing your proper role. Worry not that no one knows of you; seek to be worth knowing."

14. "Let the other man do his job without your interference."

15. "Do not be swayed by personal opinion; recognize no inescapable necessity; do not be stubborn; do not be egotistic."

16. "Juniors are to be respected. How do we know that in the future they will not be our equals? If, however, at forty or fifty they have no reputation, they need no longer be respected."

17. "To be of high moral conduct when engaged in administration is to be like the North Star. As it remains in its one position, all the other stars surround it."

18. "Formerly men studied for self-improvement; today men study for the sake of appearances."

19. "It is hard to find a man who will study for three years without thinking of a post in government."

Nine Steps in Management Development

1. *Assess Development Needs.*   A management development program should be based on what the company needs now, what it will need in the future, and the skills and shortcomings of its managers and managers-in-training.

2. *Involve Top Management.*   Many development programs fail to achieve results because, although top management initially gives its blessing, there is little follow-through. Unless management is ready to welcome and utilize what participants are learning, no progress will be made and frustration will result.

3. *Obtain Participant Input.*   The program will be more effective and better received if future participants have a hand in shaping it.

4. *Establish Objectives.*   To help participants focus on the program's purpose, set up measurable objectives and evaluate the extent to which they are met.

5. *Combine Theory with Work Experience.*   The best way to learn is by doing, not by reading or sitting through lectures.

6. *Be Selective But Not Exclusive.*   Look for people who have potential; don't limit the program to a few superstars who are likely to succeed anyway. Refine your assessment program, so that "late bloomers" won't be overlooked.

7. *Implement the Program.*   It should combine on-the-job experience with off-the-job training, discussion, and enrichment.

8. *Debrief and Reinforce.*   After the program, the participants should give feedback, both to pinpoint changes that need to be made in the program and to crystalize in their minds the concepts they learned. Further, they

should be expected to apply that knowledge on a day-to-day basis.

9. *Reevaluate.* There should be an ongoing process to ascertain the program's relevance, effectiveness, and productivity.

Source: Jon English and Anthony R. Marchione, "Nine Steps in Management Development," *Business Horizons*, June 1977.

How Top Management Differs from Middle Management and Everyone Else

1. 41 percent of top managers are performers, while 42 percent of middle managers and 35 percent of the general population are.

2. 24 percent of top managers are achievers, while only 14 percent of middle managers and 8 percent of the general population are.

3. 22 percent of top managers are commanders, but only 18 percent of middle managers and 16 percent of the general population are.

4. Only 5 percent of top managers are pleasers, but 11 percent of middle managers and 14 percent of the general population are.

5. Only 4 percent of top managers are attachers, but 6 percent of middle managers and 8 percent of the general population are.

6. Only 3 percent of top managers are avoiders, but 9 percent of middle managers and 20 percent of the general population are.

Adapted from Gerald Bell, *The Achievers: Six Styles of Personality and Leadership* (Chapel Hill, N.C.: Preston-Hill, 1973).

How Middle Management Feels About Top Management

1. 87 percent feel conflicts are seldom dealt with or are dealt with inadequately.

2. 82 percent want increased job and functional status but don't know how to tell top management.

3. 71 percent don't know what top management thinks of them, are unsure of their relationship with top managers, and don't know how they are evaluated.

4. 65 percent don't know what it takes to be successful in the organization.

5. 65 percent feel that top management can't help them with communication and group relations problems.

6. 62 percent are concerned about developing a management team that can work together.

7. 59 percent think that top-management effectiveness is no better than average.

Source: Chris Argyris, "Interpersonal Barriers to Decision-Making," *Harvard Business Review*, March–April 1966.

Fourteen Ways in Which Top Business Men and Women Differ

Based on two surveys done by Korn-Ferry International, an executive search firm—one in 1979 of 1,700 senior male executives at large U.S. companies, and one in 1982 of 300 senior female executives at large U.S. companies.

1. The average age of the executive woman is 46; that of the man is 53.

2. 60 percent of the women are eldest or only children, 49 percent of the men.

3. 52 percent of the women are single, 4 percent of the men.

4. 40.7 percent of the women are married, more than 94 percent of the men.

5. Almost 7 percent of the women are separated or widowed, less than 2 percent of the men.

6. Almost 17 percent of the women have been divorced, 2.4 percent of the men.

7. 27.6 percent of the women have never been married, less than 1 percent of the men.

8. 61 percent of the women are childless, 3 percent of the men.

9. 60 percent of the women say "religion is of little or no importance" in their lives; 63 percent of the men say religion is "a moderate or significant part" of their lives.

10. 49 percent of the women are conservative on economic issues, 74 percent of the men.

11. 21 percent of the women are conservative on social issues, 42 percent of the men.

12. 20 percent of the women don't have college degrees, 8 percent of the men.

13. 30 percent of the women have graduate degrees, 43 percent of the men.

14. 21 percent of the women have relocated during their careers, 81 percent of the men.

Fifteen Companies Where CEOs Are Least Likely to Be Overpaid

When comparing CEO compensation to return on stockholders' equity, these companies had the best ratios among the top publicly owned companies in their respective industries.

1. Conglomerates: Raytheon; 3M.

2. Pharmaceuticals: Smithkline Bechman; Upjohn.

3. Office equipment: Data General.

4. Food: A. E. Staley Manufacturing.

5. Retailing: Supermarkets General; American Stores.

6. Commercial Banking: First Interstate Bank of California

7. Diversified financial: Loews; INA.

8. Oil: Amerada Hess; Standard Oil of Ohio.

9. Chemicals: NL Industries.

10. Metals: Northwest Industries.

Ten Ways to Fail as a New Company President

According to Robert Wilson, vice-chairman and former chairman of Memorex, these are the most common mistakes new company presidents make:

1. They "assume the way will be prepared" for them. They come into a company without insisting that the board indicate to everyone that they will be in control.

2. They "fail to note language differences." They overlook the fact that the words they use may not carry the same meaning for employees, and they refuse to clarify themselves or to adopt their employees' terminology.

3. They "remain invisible." They refuse to make any changes that might draw attention to themselves, especially popular ones that might set them off on the right foot with employees.

4. They "fail to get the confidence of key subordinates." They avoid them socially and never get to know them well.

5. They "fail to get the confidence of the entire organization." They refuse to go into the field to meet with employees and hear what's on their minds.

6. They "fail to distinguish between urgent and not-so-urgent problems." They make hurried or drastic decisions and pay no attention to the degree of seriousness of the issue.

7. They "don't bother to set [their] own style." They let the organization dictate how to do things rather than make sure that people know what they want done.

8. They "avoid seeing outsiders." They don't bother meeting important suppliers and customers and don't

introduce salesmen to people they know outside the company.

9. They "fail to take charge." They don't act like leaders.

10. They "forget about industrial statesmanship." They don't have basic business concepts in mind, have no faith in business as a cornerstone of society, and therefore act in an irresponsible and short-sighted manner.

Source: Robert C. Wilson, "The New Company President: Ten Steps to Failure," *Nation's Business*, December 1970.

Eight Rules for Office Workers

A list dated 1872 was discovered by a Boston officer manager upon cleaning out a file and was reprinted in the Boston Sunday Herald, *October 5, 1958.*

1. "Office employees each day will fill lamps, clean chimneys and trim wicks. Wash windows once a week."

2. "Each clerk will bring in a bucket of water and a scuttle of coal for the day's business."

3. "Make your pens carefully. You may whittle nibs to your individual taste."

4. "Men employees will be given an evening off each week for courting purposes, or two evenings a week if they go regularly to church."

5. "After thirteen hours of labor in the office, the employee should spend the remaining time reading the Bible and other good books."

6. "Every employee should lay aside from each pay day a goodly sum of his earnings for his benefit during his declining years so that he will not become a burden on society."

7. "Any employee who smokes Spanish cigars, uses liquor in any form, or frequents pool and public halls or gets shaved in a barbershop will give good reason to suspect his worth, intentions, integrity and honesty."

8. "The employee who has performed his labor faithfully and without fault for five years will be given an increase of five cents per day in his pay, providing profits from business permit it."

Nine Reasons People Gossip

1. To spread information that management wants known but doesn't want to sanction officially.

2. To assess the informal power structure within the organization.

3. As an early warning system—a way to let co-workers know when management is receptive to their ideas and when it is not.

4. To double-check personal observations by hearing what others have to say.

5. To promote group bonding within the organization.

6. To share information across organizational status lines.

7. To study organizational communication networks.

8. To convey bad news.

9. To test reaction to an idea before taking official action on it.

Fifteen Facts About Office Romances

1. 77 percent of all couples work together in some capacity, and 63 percent work next to or near each other.

2. 94 percent of the women and 84 percent of the men involved are considered to be average or better than average in appearance.

3. 74 percent of the women are subordinate to their male lovers, and 48 percent of them are secretaries.

4. Office relationships cause considerable gossip 70 percent of the time.

5. 72 percent of the men and 60 percent of the women display favoritism toward their lovers.

6. 55 percent of both men and women receive advice on the affair from colleagues.

7. 33 percent of the men's superiors and 38 percent of the women's don't know what to do about the situation.

8. 16 percent of the men's subordinates and 10 percent of the women's quit over the matter.

9. 24 percent of the men promote their lovers.

10. 14 percent of the women flaunt their new power.

11. 25 percent of the men and 28 percent of the women become easier to get along with.

12. 24 percent of both men and women begin keeping shorter hours.

13. 18 percent of both men and women are defended by colleagues.

14. 7.5 percent of the women are threatened or blackmailed by colleagues.

15. 12 percent of the men and 6 percent of the women are reprimanded by their superiors.

Source: Robert E. Quinn, "Coping with Cupid: The Formation, Impact, and Management of Romantic Relationships in Organizations," *Administrative Science Quarterly*, March 1977.

Mary Cunningham on Women and Business

Mary Cunningham former vice-president of strategic planning and project development at Seagram, became famous as the woman who rose very quickly at Bendix Corporation. She has been quoted as saying:

1. "[Rumors, gossip, and innuendos are] a weapon used against successful women to undermine their credibility. . . ."

2. "It would seem that many people have no framework for understanding a woman who sets a record in business—so they turn to the shopworn explanation that she used her sexual charms to get there."

3. "People have a tendency, particularly with women advisers, to fall prey to the Garden of Eden psychology that they somehow have undue influence over the man."

4. ". . . at some point the concern for appearances compromises performance—and it is exactly at that point that I believe a woman must say, 'Stop.'"

5. "I think the wives of chairmen historically have been seriously undervalued. . . . There's a misconception out there that the woman is influencing the decision and somehow that's not macho."

6. "Is it not possible that we have not yet discovered the effectiveness of male-female teams whose emotional and spiritual compatibility only enhances their intellectual creativity as a unit?"

7. "Many people don't understand the dynamism, excitement, and energy that can be generated by two people who are totally supportive."

8. "[Employers] must channel more women into line responsibilities instead of pointing them—or letting them point themselves—toward staff jobs."

9. "... employers must give women some of the difficult assignments—not 'protect' them by reserving them for the routine or easy jobs."

What People in Organizations Think of Office Politics

Based on a survey of 428 people.

1. Common in most organizations: 93 percent.

2. "Successful executives must be 'good politicians'": 89 percent.

3. "Powerful executives act politically": 74 percent.

4. "You have to be political to get ahead": 70 percent.

5. It produces conflict: 70 percent.

6. Common at work: 69 percent.

7. "Only organizationally weak people play politics": 68 percent.

8. Unfair: 63 percent.

9. A lack of it makes for a happier organization: 60 percent.

10. Unhealthy: 56 percent.

11. Bad: 55 percent.

12. Irrational: 55 percent.

13. Results in inefficiency: 55 percent.

14. "Top management should try to get rid of politics": 49 percent.

15. "Sometimes clean and sometimes dirty": 36 percent.

16. "Sometimes good and sometimes bad": 31 percent.

17. "Sometimes necessary and sometimes not": 28 percent.

18. Necessary: 28 percent.

19. Sometimes necessary: 28 percent.

20. "At least sometimes common" at work: 19 percent.

NOTE: There is a significant correlation (− .29) between a high level of satisfaction with one's job and the tendency to see less politics in the workplace and feel that it isn't necessarily a bad thing. Conversely, it is those who are the most dissatisfied who perceive things as negatively political.

Source: Victor Murray and Jeffrey Gandz, "Games Executives Play: Politics at Work," *Business Horizons*, December 1980.

Eight Power Indicators

Managers have power if:

1. They can help someone on the outs with the company.

2. They can get good jobs for those under them.

3. They can get good raises for those under them.

4. They can get their concerns aired at meetings.

5. They are allowed to go over budget.

6. They can get to top management quickly.

7. They can get to top management frequently.

8. They are kept informed about plans and decisions as they occur.

Adapted from Rosabeth Moss Kanter, "Power Failures in Management Circuits," *Harvard Business Review*, July–August 1979.

Michael Korda's List of Powerful Americans

Asked by a magazine to list America's most powerful people, Michael Korda, editor-in-chief of Simon & Schuster and author of the best-selling book Power, *wrote that there were few examples today and then proceeded to cite a number of men (both dead and alive) who had power in the past.*

1. J. Edgar Hoover as director of the FBI.

2. Henry Kissinger as secretary of state.

3. David Rockefeller as chairman of Chase Manhattan Bank.

4. Nelson Rockefeller as governor of New York.

5. Henry Luce as chairman of Time, Inc.

6. William S. Paley as chairman of CBS.

7. Richard Daley as mayor of Chicago.

8. Henry Ford II as chairman of Ford Motor Company.

9. Averell Harriman as Democratic Party elder statesman.

10. George Meany as president of the AFL-CIO.

11. Jimmy Hoffa as president of the International Brotherhood of Teamsters.

12. General David Sarnoff as chairman of RCA.

13. Cardinal Spellman as archbishop of New York.

14. Robert Moses as chairman of the Triborough Bridge and NYC Tunnel Authority in New York.

15. Harold Geneen as chairman of ITT.

16. H. L. Hunt as rich oilman and political conservative.

17. John Paul Getty as another rich oilman.

18. Juan Trippe as founder and president of Pan Am.

19. Charles Revson as founder and president of Revlon.

20. Frank Stanton as president of CBS.

Source: Michael Korda, "The Gradual Decline and Total Collapse of Nearly Everyone," *Family Weekly*, August 29, 1982.

Past and Present Members of the Trilateral Commission

Until Jimmy Carter became president of the United States, few people had heard of the Trilateral Commission and even fewer cared about it. But when charges of conspiracy to manipulate politics and economics began to surface, interest in the organization grew.

Founded in 1973 by Chase Manhattan Bank Chairman David Rockefeller, the commission was created to bring together some 300 international movers and shakers to further cooperation between nations and geographic regions. Some of the people who have been associated with it are:

1. I. W. Abel, former president of United Steelworkers of America

2. Ernest C. Arbuckle, former chairman of Wells Fargo Bank

3. Anne Armstrong, ambassador to Great Britain and co-chairman of the 1980 Reagan-Bush Campaign

4. John Paul Austin, former chairman of Coca-Cola Co.

5. George W. Ball, former undersecretary of state and former chairman of Lehman Brothers, Inc.

6. W. Michael Blumenthal, chairman of Burroughs Corp.

7. William E. Brock, U.S. trade representative and former chairman of the Republican National Committee

8. Harold Brown, former secretary of defense

9. Zbigniew Brzezinski, former National Security Council adviser

10. John F. Burlingame, vice-chairman of General Electric Co.

11. Arthur F. Burns, former chairman of the Federal Reserve System

12. George Bush, U.S. vice-president

13. Philip Caldwell, chairman of Ford Motor Co.

14. Jimmy Carter, former U.S. president

15. Sol Chaikin, president of the International Ladies Garment Workers Union

16. Alden W. Clausen, former president of the World Bank, and former president of Bank of America

17. John Cowles, Jr., former chairman of Minneapolis Star and Tribune Co.

18. Alan Cranston, U.S. senator from California

19. John H. Glenn, Jr., U.S. senator from Ohio

20. Patrick E. Haggerty, honorary chairman of Texas Instruments, Inc.

21. Philip M. Hawley, president and CEO of Carter Hawley Hale Stores, Inc.

22. Walter W. Heller, professor of economics at the University of Minnesota, Minneapolis

23. William A. Hewitt, chairman of Deere & Co.

24. Carla A. Hills, former secretary of housing and urban development

25. J. K. Jamieson, former chairman of Exxon Co.

26. Edgar F. Kaiser, chairman emeritus of Kaiser Industries Corp.

27. Edgar F. Kaiser, Jr., former chairman of Kaiser Steel Corp.

28. Lane Kirkland, president of the AFL-CIO

29. Henry A. Kissinger, former secretary of state

30. Wilber D. Mills, former chairman of the House Ways and Means Committee

31. Walter F. Mondale, former U.S. vice-president

32. Lee L. Morgan, chairman and CEO of Caterpillar Tractor Co.

33. William R. Pearce, vice-president of Cargill, Inc.

34. John H. Perkins, president of Continental Illinois National Bank and Trust Co.

35. Peter G. Peterson, chairman of Lehman Brothers Kuhn Loeb, Inc.

36. Edwin O. Reischauer, former ambassador to Japan

37. Elliot L. Richardson, former U.S. attorney general, secretary of defense, and secretary of health, education, and welfare

38. David Rockefeller, former chairman of Chase Manhattan Bank

39. John D. Rockefeller IV, governor of West Virgina

40. Mark Shepherd, Jr., chairman of Texas Instruments, Inc.

41. Edson W. Spencer, chairman and CEO of Honeywell, Inc.

42. Arthur R. Taylor, former president of CBS, Inc.

43. James R. Thompson, governor of Illinois

44. Russell E. Train, president of the World Wildlife Fund—U.S.

45. Cyrus R. Vance, former secretary of state

46. Paul A. Volcker, chairman of the Federal Reserve System

47. Caspar W. Weinberger, secretary of defense

48. Thorton A. Wilson, former chairman of Boeing Co.

49. Leonard Woodcock, former president of the United Automobile Workers

50. Andrew Young, former ambassador to the United Nations

4

TECHNIQUES

Successful Ideas and Tactics

Thirty Negotiating Tactics

1. Try to gain an advantage over the opposition by planting your ideas in their minds before they reach the negotiating table.

2. Try to catch them off-guard by doing what you want and then announcing it at the start of the negotiations.

3. Try to use your first-strike capability by hitting them with an ultimatum rather than an offer to talk.

4. Try to force them into agreeing with you quickly by taking immediate action against them, rather than waiting until negotiations are set up.

5. Try to ensure success in the negotiations by reducing the areas of disagreement.

6. Attempt to gain control of the negotiations by dealing with one issue at a time.

7. Begin by asking for everything you want in hopes that they'll agree to at least a few of your demands.

8. Begin by asking for a great deal in order to overwhelm them.

9. Ask for the opposite of what you really want on the assumption that they will respond contrarily.

89

10. Try to create momentum in your favor by beginning with the demands you can most easily win.

11. Be vague about what you want to keep them from developing a counterstrategy.

12. Offer them something you know they want in return for what you want.

13. Offer to make concessions in areas that are in fact of little concern to you.

14. Create false demands solely for the purpose of giving them up as a trade-off.

15. Let them think they've won and then ask for a small concession.

16. Let them think it's in their best interests to do what you want.

17. Suggest that you represent a great deal of power in order to intimidate them.

18. Bring powerful or influential people with you to bolster your image of strength.

19. Let others represent you at the negotiations so they can say things that you might refrain from saying because it could hurt or weaken your image.

20. Make demands you know they can't meet and will back away from to show your aggressive position.

21. Force them to drop out of the negotiations by escalating your demands far beyond any point they are prepared to meet.

22. Change your tactics unexpectedly to throw them off-guard.

23. Have a secret plan you can exercise at the last minute if necessary.

24. Mislead them by bluffing or distorting the facts.

25. Drag out the negotiations in hopes of wearing them down.

26. Weaken their resolve by saying very little.

27. Leave the negotiations unexpectedly in order to throw them off-guard and to suggest your lack of interest.

28. Attempt to pressure them into dealing with you by refusing to discuss the matter much longer.

29. Depend on several different people with several different styles to present your case, alternating back and forth between them as suits the discussion.

30. If you've lost most of your demands, suggest that they grant you at least one or two as a measure of good faith.

Seven Ways to Deal with Creative People

1. Provide them with as much information about the job they are to do as you can.

2. Don't isolate them. They may need quiet time to create, but they also need to feel a part of the team and must be a part of the team.

3. Give them enough time to do their jobs. Don't expect wonderful ideas on a moment's notice. A few people do their best work under pressure, but most don't.

4. Avoid criticizing their work if you're not going to make the final decision on it. And even if you are, be careful how you do it. Be as specific as you can about the problem and allow them to try again.

5. Don't dwell on details. If the general direction of their work is good, give positive reinforcement first and then suggest revisions.

6. Allow them the freedom to be moody. It goes with the territory.

7. Above all, be supportive.

Nine Employee Put-Downs to Be Avoided

1. *"The Peremptory Summons."*   Telling an employee you need to see him immediately. Rarely are you summoning him for a true emergency. More often than not, you are annoyed with him and want to let him know it, oblivious to the demands of his job, or you are merely pulling rank. He will come, but he'll arrive either anxious, resentful, or annoyed with you. You've disrupted his day, and he's probably unprepared to deal with whatever problem you spring on him.

2. *"Improper Address."*   Calling an employee by his last name or "Hey, you." It's an impersonal gesture and reminds him of his lack of status in the organization.

3. *"Inaccessibility."*   Always being too busy to see or talk to an employee. You make him feel as if he is imposing on your time, even though one of your responsibilities is to maintain communication with your subordinates.

4. *"Blame Passing."*   Implying that an employee caused a problem that was primarily your responsibility. You demand an explanation for an incident beyond his control or stress the consequences of a problem even though he is in no position to do anything about it.

5. *"Procrastination."*   Delaying feedback on a matter important to the employee. Rather than admitting you can't or won't make a decision, you send the employee back to do more research or to prepare a more detailed report, implying that the delay is due to lack of preparation on his part.

6. *"Asking for Obscure Details."*   Browbeating an employee by asking for information you know he either doesn't have or will have to take great pains to find or communicate. It's unproductive and makes him feel inadequate.

7. *"Public Reprimands."*   Criticizing an employee in front of co-workers and subordinates. It is provocative and demoralizing.

8. *"Inattentiveness."*   Showing obvious disinterest when an employee is trying to talk to you. He learns that you are not a person to confide in and will no longer bring you potentially important information.

9. *"Impatience."*   Abruptly cutting off an employee. You show a lack of concern and imply that your feelings and emotions are more important than his.

Adapted from William R. Tracey, "Put-Down Techniques: Are You Guilty of Them?" *Personnel Journal*, May 1979.

Eight Steps in Disciplining an Employee

1. When you see or know about employee misconduct, arrange a private meeting with the individual. Don't reprimand him in public and don't pull him out of a group or the middle of a project without warning. But do meet with him as soon after the incident as you can.

2. Have all the facts, and then be specific about the problem. Explain the situation and why you are concerned about it.

3. Give him time to respond, and listen to what he has to say.

4. Agree on future behavior. Either work out a solution with him or at least make sure he understands what you expect from him.

5. Reinforce positive behavior when you see it. If you see that he has made changes, let him know.

6. If the problem has not been corrected, send him a letter of reprimand. This indicates the seriousness of the problem and also commits the incident to record, which you may need to refer to if a dismissal results and is contested. Include facts about the incident, corporate policy on the matter, past discussions you've had with the employee, and future actions you will take if necessary.

7. If the problem still continues, a suspension of several days (long enough to make an impression) is in order.

8. If the problem still continues, dismissal is in order. But first a hearing should be conducted to make sure the employee's side has been heard and that management did not handle the incident in an arbitrary manner.

Nine Types of Office Troublemakers

According to management consultant Robert M. Bramson, who has studied over 400 managers and workers in a variety of organizations, 10 percent are troublemakers.

1. *Sherman Tank.* A hostile-aggressive who runs over people with his loudly stated opinions. Be direct with him. Give your opinion on the matter, then wait for him to blow off steam.

2. *Sniper.* Another hostile-aggressive who depends on sarcasm to express dissatisfaction. Draw him out and encourage him to express his true feelings.

3. *Exploder.* A third hostile-aggressive who is disruptive with extreme expressions of emotion. Ignore him when he does this.

4. *Complainer.* He wants an audience while he lists everything that's wrong. Use reflective listening by paraphrasing his complaints and making noncommittal acknowledging sounds ("ums" and "ahs").

5. *Analyst.* An indecisive who worries about making mistakes. He needs verification of every decision and deadline.

6. *Be-Nicer.* Another indecisive who worries about making enemies. Draw out his opinion without giving away your own and ask him what's best for the company.

7. *Unresponsive.* Someone who won't say anything. Say nothing yourself while you sit expectantly, awaiting a reply.

8. *Real Expert.* A know-it-all who is often right but doesn't see his errors the rest of the time. Help him by asking about the results and consequences of his ideas.

9. *Phony Expert.* A know-it-all who seldom has the right answers. Use an approach similar to the one for the real expert, helping him use logic to come up with a better plan.

How to Train a Successor

1. From day one, know what your company expects of you. Are you supposed to train a replacement, to make recommendations, or to leave the matter to the personnel department? Knowing all of this will give you an idea of how much time and effort you need to spend grooming a successor.

2. Keep in mind that what you are told doesn't always reflect what really happens. You may be told you will be able to choose your successor, but in the end someone else may have control over the matter.

3. Also keep in mind that a company's succession policies may change with the health of the company. If all is going well, your superiors will be happy to have you choose a successor, but if there's trouble, especially in your area of responsibility, they may take that privilege away from you.

4. Don't wait too long before readying a successor. You may be told you won't be promoted until you have a replacement.

5. On the other hand, if you train a replacement before you know you're going anywhere, you may work yourself out of a job if it appears your department is overstaffed.

6. When considering a replacement, see who is available within your company before looking elsewhere.

Morale will stay higher if people know you are willing to train someone inexperienced but already working there than if you insist on bringing in an already qualified individual from another company.

7. Don't look for a carbon copy of yourself. Consider what the job will require in the future, not what you were able to do in the past.

8. Get feedback from others before making your decision. Ask them what kind of person they think the job needs. They will often have a better perspective than you have.

9. During the transition period, make sure you don't linger over your successor too long, that you don't duplicate each other's work, and that you each have specific duties and responsibilities.

10. Don't sabotage your successor. You may unconsciously want to guarantee that no one ever does as well in the job as you did.

11. Think of choosing your successor as simply another job responsibility, to be done with as much professionalism and care as everything else you have done while holding that position.

Eight Rules for Getting the Most Out of Your Telephone

1. Avoid calling people around 11 A.M. (their time) and 3 P.M., the two peak times for telephone usage.

2. If you can't get past the secretary, try calling either early in the morning or after working hours, times when you're likely to find the person you're calling alone.

3. Organize your thoughts before calling and write them down if necessary. (Three-by-five index cards work well.)

4. Begin by stating who you are (giving not only your name, but also your company, position, and any previous contact you've had if there's any chance you might not be remembered). If you don't, you run the risk of embarrassing both yourself and the other person and of wasting time with explanations.

5. Unless your business is brief (under five minutes), assume you'll be setting up a future time to talk. State how much time you think you'll need and ask if he is free to discuss the matter now or would rather have you call back. One exception: When you know he'll try to avoid you, state your case while you have him on the phone. You may never have another chance.

6. Be concise, and speak rapidly but clearly. People tend to talk too slowly on the phone.

7. Steer clear of discussing controversial subjects over the phone unless you're easily intimidated, in which case you're better off covering them now than in person. In most instances you want to watch the other person's reactions when bringing up a stressful topic, but if you're unsure of yourself, you may prefer the impersonality of the phone.

8. If you've never met in person but soon will, avoid becoming too familiar over the phone. Don't give him the chance to form a mental picture of you based on your phone personality. If what he sees doesn't fit his preconceived idea, he may find working with you distracting and unsettling.

Twelve Essentials for
Good Presentations

1. When possible, hold presentations in your conference room rather than in your client's.

2. When you must use an unfamiliar facility, check it out beforehand, preferably allowing enough time to make changes in your audiovisual equipment if necessary. Learn where the electrical outlets are, how the lighting works, how good the acoustics are, and where you can prop up your displays.

3. Know your responsibilities to your audience: Are you expected to provide refreshments, ashtrays, and notepads?

4. Keep audiovisual aid to a minimum if you can't handle them. Presentations allow others to size you up, and if you look like a klutz in the process, you'll do yourself more harm than good.

5. If you use slides, keep them simple and easy to read. Use them only to illustrate main ideas. If it is necessary to go into greater detail, hand out printed supplements.

6. Tailor the presentation to meet the needs of and to influence the person in the audience most responsible for passing judgment on your ideas, rather than trying to entertain and impress everyone equally.

7. A crisp and formal style is better than a chatty and informal one to keep your audience focused and to demonstrate your control over the material.

8. Begin by summarizing briefly the points you'll cover. This will prepare the audience for your material.

9. Do not read from your slides, charts, or displays. This wastes time and bores your audience. Rather, coor-

dinate your audiovisuals with your speech so that they pictorially illustrate what you are saying.

10. Don't leave up your displays when you are not referring to them. They'll only be distractions. Instead, shift to blank slides or pages between points to bring the audience's focus back to you.

11. Cover points in increasing order of importance so that you can conclude on a strong note and leave your audience thinking.

12. Pass out handouts after you've finished speaking, so your audience won't be reading and shuffling them about during your speech.

Six Writing Styles

John S. Fielden, professor of management communication at the University of Alabama and managing partner of Fielden Associates, suggests that one of the following styles is suitable for business correspondence:

1. *Forceful Style.* For when you have real power in the situation. Use the active voice (the subject performing the action of the verb rather than being acted upon), say what you mean, and avoid hedging your points with modifying words and phrases.

2. *Passive Style.* For bad news and when addressing a superior. Use the passive voice, don't give orders, avoid using "I" when making negative statements (use "others" or "some people" instead), tone down ideas with modifiers, and make sentences ponderous to blunt bad news and slow down the reader.

3. *Personal Style*.   For good news and when trying to persuade. Use the active voice with lots of "I"s, personal names, contractions, direct questions, short sentences, and personal thoughts and references.

4. *Impersonal Style*.   For technical writing. Keep references to people to a minimum and use titles or job descriptions rather than names. Keep yourself out of the writing by using the passive voice, and make sentences complex.

5. *Colorful Style*.   For advertising and sale letters. Add color through adjectives, adverbs, metaphors, and similes.

6. *Less Colorful Style*.   For ordinary business writing. Cut out adjectives, adverbs, metaphors, and figures of speech; use a combination of impersonal and passive styles; and "remove any semblance of wit, liveliness, and vigor from the writing."

Source: John S. Fielden, "'What Do You Mean You Don't Like My Style?'" *Harvard Business Review*, May–June 1982.

Nine Ways to Get the Most Out of Conventions

1. Select which conventions to go to according to the people who will be attending and speaking, not according to the topics to be discussed.

2. Steer clear of vacation-type conventions (those that break in the afternoons for golf, tennis, skiing, etc.) unless you're primarily interested in having some tax-deductible R & R. The more conventioneers are spread out by activities, the less chance you'll have to make

contact with them. (One exception: If you're particularly good at a sport and know you'll impress an important executive who'll be there, the trip might be worth your while.)

3. If given a choice, attend several smaller conventions rather than one colossal one. (But don't lower your sights when it comes to the people you want to meet. Search out small but selective gatherings.)

4. Stay in the main hotel; don't try to economize by staying in a cheaper one a few blocks away. You'll miss impromptu meetings if you're not always on the scene.

5. Attend conventions alone if possible. If you travel with family or co-workers, you'll be tempted to spend your free time with them instead of mingling.

6. Choose small sessions over big ones.

7. Avoid sessions where audience participation and discussion will be kept to a minimum.

8. Don't follow schedules rigidly. Cut sessions if you've been asked to join a valuable contact for coffee or drinks.

9. Leave the convention with at least one new contact and follow up on it afterward.

Six Ways to Meet Important People at Conventions

1. Learn to recognize them so you'll be ready to strike up a conversation when the opportunity arises.

2. Approach them at times when they're a captive audience—when they are standing alone in registration or checkout lines, waiting for elevators or cabs, and so on. Then be friendly but not overly aggressive.

3. Rescue them from embarrassing situations at autograph parties. An author waiting to sign books will be grateful to have you to talk to. Hang around the table until the session is over and then suggest continuing your conversation elsewhere. (Never confess, however, that you haven't read anything he's written.)

4. Try joining them at meals. Often no plans have been made for them and they end up sitting alone. If that's the case, go up to their table, ask if anyone will be joining them, and, if not, ask if you can sit down. Seldom will you be refused.

5. After sessions ask them questions about the material they've covered. Show some interest and suggest continuing the conversation elsewhere.

6. Offer to show them the sights in town. This works if you're more familiar with the area than they are or if you have a means of transportation and they don't. Frequently such people have seen more hotels and convention rooms than they care to remember and would love the chance to get away for a while.

The Big Five Washington Lobbyists

1. *Patton, Boggs & Blow.*   The law firm of Tom Boggs, son of the late Hale Boggs. It has strong Democratic contacts and is known especially for fund-raising parties. The fee is $250 an hour, and clients include American Express, the Sultanate of Oman, and Marathon Oil.

2. *Gray and Co.*   The firm of Robert Gray, head of public relations firm Hill and Knowlton's Washington office until Reagan came to town. Gray has had strong ties to the Republican party since he was secretary to the cabinet during the Eisenhower administration and is now the lobbyist of choice for those dealing with the Reagan administration. The fee is $350 an hour.

3. *Charls Walker Associates.*   Another lobbyist with Republican ties, Charls E. Walker worked in the Treasury Department for both the Eisenhower and the Nixon administrations. His specialties are taxation and finance. The fee is calculated on a retainer basis depending on the project's size and length. Clients include Ford, General Electric, Alcoa, and Procter & Gamble.

4. *Williams & Jensen.*   Jerry Don Williams's law firm. Williams has Democratic ties from the Hubert Humphrey days and is known for his Oklahoma demeanor.

5. *Timmons and Co.*   A law firm founded by five Nixon administration Republicans. Fees run over $200,000 per client. Clients include ABC, Standard Oil of Indiana, and Eastern Airlines.

Source: Sandra McElwaine, "The Super Lobbyists," *Family Weekly*, January 30, 1983.

The Top Business and Professional Political
Action Committees

1. National Association of Realtors PAC

2. American Medical Association PAC

3. United Automobile Workers UAW-V-CAP

4. Machinists Non-Partisan Political League

5. National Education Association PAC

6. American Medical Association (California) PAC

7. American Bankers Association BANKPAC

8. National Association of Home Builders PAC

9. Associated Milk Producers PAC

10. Automobile and Truck Dealers Election Action Committee

11. AFL-CIO COPE Political Contributions Committee

12. American Medical Association (Texas) PAC

13. Seafarers Political Activity Donation

14. National Association of Life Underwriters PAC

15. Engineers Political Education Committee (Operating Engineers)

16. Associated General Contractors PAC

17. Active Ballot Clue (Food & Commercial Workers)

18. National Rifle Association Political Victory Fund

19. United Steelworkers of America PAC

20. American Dental PAC

21. Communications Workers of America—COPE Political Contributions Committee

22. International Ladies Garment Workers Union Campaign Committee

23. Chicago Mercantile Exchange PAC

24. Sheetmetal Workers' International Association Political Action League

25. American Medical Association (Florida) PAC

26. Association of Trial Lawyers of America

27. Responsible Citizens Political League (Railway, Airline & Steamship Clerks)

28. Independent Insurance Agents of America PAC

How Sales Reps and Engineering Managers View Time-Wasters

1. Sales reps say telephone interruptions are their number-one problem; it's only the third worst problem for engineering managers.

2. Sales reps say drop-in visitors are their second worst problem; they rank ninth with engineering managers.

3. Sales reps blame lack of discipline as the third biggest time-waster in their jobs; it ranks at the bottom for engineering managers.

4. Sales reps rank crises fourth; engineering managers rank them sixth.

5. Sales reps find meetings the fifth worst offender; engineering managers rank them fourth.

6. Sales reps say the sixth cause of loss of time is problems with setting goals and priorities and meeting deadlines; engineering managers don't consider them major problems at all.

7. Sales reps rank indecision and procrastination seventh; engineering managers rank them eighth.

8. Sales reps find trying to do too much is the eighth worst cause of lost time; engineering managers don't find it a major problem.

9. Sales reps say unfinished tasks are the next-to-last major cause of lost time; engineering managers rank them seventh.

10. Sales reps find unclear communication is the least major cause of wasted time; it's the fifth worst problem for engineering managers.

11. Sales reps don't even mention faulty or late information as a problem; it's number one by engineering managers.

12. Sales reps don't mention delegation problems either; it's ranked number two by engineering managers.

Adapted from Michael LeBoeuf, "Managing Time Means Managing Yourself," *Business Horizons*, February 1980.

5

THE MARKETPLACE

Ads, Markets, and Products

What You Need to Know to Make Your Advertising Effective

1. How is your product different from the competition's?

2. How is it similar?

3. Who buys it?

4. Why do they buy it?

5. How often do they buy it?

6. Who uses it?

7. Where do they use it?

8. How do they use it?

9. What does it make them feel like?

10. Where do they buy it?

11. When do they buy it?

12. Who pays for it?

13. How do they pay for it?

14. Who sells it?

Consumer Use of Advertising Media

One of the factors in deciding which advertising medium to use is the length of time the consumer is exposed to your message. The average consumer:

1. Watches television 6 hours and 44 minutes a day.

2. Listens to the radio 3 hours and 24 minutes a day if a man, 3 hours and 29 minutes a day if a woman.

3. Reads a magazine a total of 93 minutes.

4. Reads a newspaper a total of 34 minutes.

5. Sees a billboard 31 times a month.

6. Sits in front of transit signs 22.7 minutes each ride.

7. Use the Yellow Pages 43.9 times a year.

Seven Types of Television Commercials

1. *Demonstration.* Shows the consumer how to use the product and what its benefits are.

2. *Testimonials*. Enhances the product's credibility because real people tell why they like it.

3. *Spokesperson*.   Uses an individual to sell the product. Corporate employees, character actors, or celebrities may be used. Celebrities help viewers remember the commercials, but they don't motivate them to switch brands.

4. *Slice-of-Life*. Shows the product being used in a realistic situation to increase viewer identification with the product and its users.

5. *Animation*.   Uses cartoons to sell the product and is an effective way to reach children, but not adults.

6. *Problem-Solution*.   Begins with a problem many viewers have and then shows how the product can help.

7. *Humor*.   Seeks to sell the product by entertaining the viewer.

Ten Products with Memorable Ads

Each year Video Storyboard Tests surveys thousands of people to find out which ads they remember and enjoyed. Based on an average of polls conducted in 1980, 1981, and 1982, these products placed the highest:

1. Miller Lite

2. Coca-Cola

3. Pepsi

4. McDonald's

5. Dr. Pepper

6. Polaroid

7. Bell System

8. Oscar Mayer

9. 7-Up

10. Life cereal

Source: Bill Abrams, "Miller Lite's Ads Best Liked, But Aren't Most Efficient," *The Wall Street Journal*, March 3, 1983.

The Ten Products with the Most Efficient Advertising

By comparing the number of people who remembered an ad to the amount of money spent on advertising, Video Storyboard was able to calculate the cost per 1,000 people reached:

1. Oscar Mayer	$6.37
2. Levi's	6.81
3. Dr. Pepper	7.83
4. Coca-Cola	8.96
5. Burger King	9.08
6. 7-Up	10.00
7. French's Mustard	10.16

8. Pepsi	10.35
9. Shasta	11.33
10. McDonald's	11.50

Source: Bill Abrams, "Miller Lite's Ads Best Liked, But Aren't Most Efficient," *The Wall Street Journal*, March 3, 1983.

Eight Regional Differences in Consumer Food Preferences

1. Fruit-flavored breakfast drinks are most popular in the South and least popular in the Pacific and Northeast regions.

2. Soft drinks are most popular in the South and least popular in the northern Plains and Pacific Northwest.

3. Wine is most popular on the West Coast and least popular in the South and Plains. Beer is most popular in the Southwest.

4. Italian food is most popular in the East, Midwest, and South, but in the West it comes in third behind Mexican and Chinese foods.

5. Dry salad dressing is popular only on the West Coast.

6. Meat and potatoes are staples in the Midwest, ethnic foods are big in the East, new and fad foods take off on the West Coast, and national brands are snapped up in the South.

7. Hard candy is most popular in the Northwest, where dark and bitter chocolates are also big. (Specifically, Pittsburghers like their chocolate solid and New Jer-

seyians like theirs in chunks.) People on the West Coast don't care for hard candy, but do like chocolate-covered cherries and milk chocolate. (San Franciscans are partial to cream fillings, while Angelenos like all kinds of chocolates.) Midwesterners don't like hard candy and do like milk chocolate. (Chicagoans like candies with nuts as well.) Southerners are in the middle as far as hard candy goes. (Floridians go for sesame candies, and those from New Orleans like Heavenly Hash and chocolate bars.)

8. In the Southeast people like their barbecue made with pork; in Texas it's made with beef; in west Texas and New Mexico it's made with kid; and in the North barbecue is any kind of meat with barbecue sauce on it.

Eleven Ways to Market to Minorities

1. Concentrate your efforts in localized areas with large minority populations (Chinatown, Harlem, Texas border towns).

2. Be prepared to do your own market research because very little information is available.

3. Know who your audience is. Don't assume all Orientals or all Hispanics, for example, share the same backgrounds. Within each minority are separate subgroups with distinct identities.

4. Tailor your ads specifically for your audience. Don't try to use mass market campaigns.

5. Don't use stereotypes in your ads.

6. Do incorporate positive cultural symbols (black heritage, Spanish culture, and so on) if appropriate to the campaign.

7. Use colloquialisms, but use them correctly.

8. Work through established networks. Win support from and advertise through local churches, social clubs, and so on.

9. Win brand loyalty through goodwill efforts such as scholarships, festivals, contests, and so on.

10. Work with retailers, defining the market you are after and showing them how they can best display your products.

11. Take the minority market seriously.

Six Products That Cannot Be Pitched with Humor

Based on research conducted by McCollum, Spielman & Co., an advertising-testing firm.

1. Medicines

2. Financial services

3. Appliances

4. Coffee

5. Cars

6. Dog food

Source: *The Wall Street Journal*, October 21, 1982.

Eight Ways to Offend the Consumer Through Advertising

Based on what people say they don't like about ads.

1. Advertise offensive, embarrassing, or for-adults-only products.

2. Make sure the ad is in bad taste.

3. Talk down to the consumer.

4. Depend on exaggeration to sell your product.

5. Lie.

6. Bombard the consumer with your ads.

7. Bore the consumer.

8. Stay away from realism.

Six Ways to Entertain the Consumer Through Advertising

Based on what people say they enjoy about ads.

1. Direct your ads to consumers you've already won over.

2. Involve the consumer in your ads.

3. Use catchy jingles and pleasing music.

4. Make your ad a quality production.

5. Make sure your ad looks good.

6. Use humor.

Eight Ways to Inform the Consumer Through Advertising

Based on which ads people say they learn from.

1. Involve the consumer in your ads.

2. Advertise products that have value or interest.

3. List your product's advantages.

4. Explain how your product works.

5. Explain what kinds of products you have available.

6. Direct your ads to consumers you've already won over.

7. Be persuasive.

8. Tell how much your product costs.

Twelve Ways to Make Your Ads More Credible

1. Don't make claims you don't back up in the ad.

2. Only use testimonials from people whose opinion can be respected.

3. Suggest that your product is widely accepted.

4. Sell your product in positive terms.

5. Avoid excessive use of adjectives.

6. Don't suggest your product is more important to the consumer than it really is.

7. Admit that your product is not perfect.

8. Avoid using jargon.

9. Use a personal tone when giving simple directions to the consumer.

10. Depending on the product, either downplay sophistication or use it effectively.

11. Use the word "new" only in comparison with some past product.

12. Use humor only when it is appropriate to your product.

Adapted from H. Gordon Lewis, *How to Make Your Advertising Twice as Effective at Half the Cost* (Chicago: Nelson-Hall, 1979).

Eight Kinds of Female Consumers

Based on research done by the Consumer Research Panels.

1. "The self-righteous social conformist"

2. "The family-oriented churchgoer"

3. "The downtrodden salvation seeker"

4. "The happy materialist"

5. "The blithe-spirited natural woman"

6. "The romance and beauty seeker"

7. "The fulfilled matron"

8. "The liberated career seeker"

Source: "The New Six in Media Research," *Media Decision*, May 1973.

Eight Kinds of Male Consumers

Based on research done by the Consumer Research Panels.

1. "The inconspicuous social isolate"

2. "The silent conservative"

3. "The embittered resigned worker"

4. "The highbrow puritan"

5. "The rebellious pleasure seeker"

6. "The work-hard play-hard executive"

7. "The masculine hero emulator"

8. "The sophisticated cosmopolitan"

Source: "The New Six in Media Research," *Media Decision*, May 1973.

Seven Facts About
the Affluent

According to studies done by Monroe Mendelsohn Research, affluent adults—those in households making at least $40,000 annually—represent 7.3 percent of the population and have and do the following:

1. The average home of an affluent is worth $149,000.

2. The average portfolio of an affluent contains $154,000 in securities.

3. The average household income of an affluent is $67,425.

4. Affluents buy 69 percent of all domestic airline tickets and 66 percent of all traveler's checks.

5. Affluents drink 45 percent of the wine and average 11.4 alcoholic drinks a week. (In addition, other studies show that 24 percent of all top executives drink beer with lunch daily.)

6. Affluents spend four times as much money on books, twelve times as much on stereo equipment, and two and a half times as much on athletic equipment as nonaffluents.

7. Affluents have guests over 2.4 times a month and take guests out 2.5 times a month.

Source: *The Wall Street Journal*, March 12, 1981.

Nine Types of Consumers

The market research firm of SRI International groups consumers into nine classifications:

1. *Belongers.* 35 percent of the population. They are outer-driven because they are concerned with their impression on others. They are conservative, traditional, and nonexperimental consumers.

2. *Achievers.* 22 percent of the population. They are also outer-driven. They are business and community leaders who are materialistic and who have comfortable lives.

3. *Emulators.* 9 percent of the population. They are also outer-driven. They are ambitious, upwardly mobile, and status conscious.

4. *Societally Conscious Individuals.* 9 percent of the population. They are inner-directed consumers because they buy to meet their own needs, rather than to fit in with others. They are interested in such causes as environmentalism and consumerism.

5. *Experimenters.* 7 percent of the population. They are also inner-directed. They are concerned with inner growth and naturalism.

6. *Sustainers.* 7 percent of the population. They are need-driven because their purchases are dictated by need rather than choice. They live on the edge of poverty and resent it.

7. *I-Am-Me's.* 5 percent of the population. They are another inner-directed group. They come from affluent backgrounds and are young, impulsive, and individualistic.

8. *Survivors*.   4 percent of the population. Another need-driven group. They are the old and the poor who cannot afford to buy what everyone else does.

9. *Integrateds*.   2 percent of the population. They are inner-directed. They have the success and power of the achievers along with the awareness of the other inner-directed groups.

Five Types of Bank Customers

Based on a survey of 1,900 people with bank accounts done by Lieber Attitude Research, Inc.

1. *Planners and Dealers*.   People looking for a profit. They are "optimistic, well-informed, fairly affluent" and tend to put their money in a variety of investments.

2. *Conservators*.   People looking for "service, privacy and one-stop shopping for their investments." They have planned for the future by building up large amounts of cash.

3. *The Uninvolved*.   People uncomfortable with banks. They often have money but do not plan well and "spend imprudently."

4. *Service-Seekers*.   People looking for interaction. Often widowed and with less education and less money than other bank customers, they want personalized service.

5. *Hopefuls.* People looking for financial help from a familiar institution. Many are young black women with less education and income than other bank customers.

Source: *The Wall Street Journal*, June 3, 1982.

Twenty Slogans No One Can Remember

Edward MacEwen, director of advertising at GTE Corporation, created a match-up quiz of corporations and their slogans. Of the 250 advertising executives who took the quiz, only 6 did better than 33 percent right. The best score was 62 percent right. Some of the slogans included were:

1. Allegheny: "Special skills for special needs."

2. Allide: "We mean business."

3. Amoco: "You expect more from a leader."

4. Bendix: "The power of ingenuity."

5. Diamond Shamrock: "The resourceful company."

6. W. R. Grace: "One step ahead of a changing world."

7. Hewlett-Packard: "When performance must be measured by results."

8. ITT: "The best ideas are the ideas that help people."

9. LTV: "Looking ahead."

10. Merrill Lynch: "A breed apart."

11. Mitel: "Building better communication."

12. Monsanto: "Without chemicals, life itself would be impossible."

13. Sears Roebuck: "You can count on Sears."

14. Sperry: "We understand how important it is to listen."

15. Stromberg-Carlson: "Communications for the information century."

16. Tektronix: "Committed to excellence."

17. 3M: "3M hears you."

18. United States Steel: "Strength you can plan on."

19. United Telecom: "A clear distinctive voice in the information age."

20. Wang: "Making the world more productive."

Source: Bill Abrams, "Understanding Through Quizzes," *The Wall Street Journal*, December 9, 1982.

The Top Ten New Products of All Time

Based on a poll of 350 research and development executives conducted by New Product Development *newsletter and listed in order of importance:*

1. Wheel

2. Bow and arrow

3. Telegraph

4. Electric light

5. Plow

6. Steam engine

7. Vaccine

8. Telephone

9. Paper

10. Flush toilet

Source: *The Wall Street Journal*, January 14, 1982.

Where New Product Ideas Come From

Consumer Products

Based on a survey of 79 new products.

1. Analysis of the competition: 38 percent.

2. Company sources other than research and development: 31.6 percent.

3. Consumer research: 17.7 percent.

4. Research and development: 13.9 percent.

5. Consumer suggestions: 12.7 percent.

6. Published information: 11.4 percent.

7. Supplier suggestions: 3.8 percent.

Industrial Products

Based on a survey of 152 new products.

1. Company sources other than research and development: 36.2 percent.

2. Analysis of the competition: 27.0 percent.

3. Research and development: 24.3 percent.

4. Product users: 15.8 percent.

5. Supplier suggestions: 12.5 percent.

6. Product user research: 10.5 percent.

7. Published information: 7.9 percent.

NOTE: percentages add to more than 100 percent because more than one source was named for some products.

Source: Leigh Lawton and A. Parasuraman, "So You Want Your New Product Planning to Be Productive," Table 1, *Business Horizons*, December 1980.

Twenty Indicators of New Product Success

Based on a survey of new product consultants conducted by New Product Development *newsletter*.

1. The project has been named.

2. The project leader has a good track record.

3. The project leader is fully committed to the project.

4. The company president has access to the project leader.

5. The project leader has a private secretary.

6. It is a new product.

7. It fulfills a corporate need.

8. It is similar to products already produced by the company.

9. It is reaching a market already familiar to the company.

10. It will have a well-known brand name on it.

11. It will have less than five models.

12. It won't need servicing or repair.

13. Purchasing it won't demand a great deal of thought and discussion.

14. At least a year has been invested in its development.

15. At least one-third of the project budget has been for research and development.

16. It will be test-marketed for at least six months.

17. At least 5 percent of projected sales will be invested in advertising.

18. Three advertising copy samples have been created.

19. The company is prepared to lose money on it for a year.

20. The product life cycle is at least ten years.

Adapted from "Twenty Clues to New-Product Success," *The Wall Street Journal*, September 24, 1981.

Seven Guidelines for Naming a Product

1. There must be some connection between the name and the product, so that the name describes or suggests what the product is or does.

2. Make sure the name works with an overall sales campaign, that it will coordinate with packaging, advertising, and public relations efforts.

3. The name must be easy to remember.

4. Use words that are pleasant to hear and say—alliteration and rhyme are often effective.

5. Make sure the name is distinctive—you don't want consumers confusing your product with someone else's.

6. The name must convey the proper image—you don't want to use masculine names for feminine products or sophisticated ones on children's merchandise.

7. Use a name that reinforces consumer expectations, that makes them feel glamorous or successful or protected.

6

===

STOCKS AND BONDS

Some Who's Whos, How Tos, and Whys

Nine Corporate Bond Ratings

1. *Standard & Poor's AAA.* The safest bond available in terms of interest and principal protection. Can be expected to fluctuate with the interest rate. Highest Grade.
   Moody's Aaa. The best quality, with low risk ensured by extremely favorable debt to equity ratio. "Gilt Edge."

2. *Standard & Poor's AA.* Only slightly less secure than the AAA bonds. High Grade.
   Moody's Aa. Very high quality, almost comparable with the Aaa bonds, but with slightly less desirable margins or less stable principal. High Grade.

3. *Standard & Poor's A.* Strong and safe, but may be affected by economic and trade conditions which may influence its selling price. Upper Medium Grade.
   Moody's A. Adequate interest and principal protection but possibly at risk in the future. Upper Medium Grade.

4. *Standard & Poor's BBB.* Can meet obligations now, given current conditions, but has little margin for adverse developments. Medium Grade.
   Moody's Baa. Adequate interest and principal protection at present, but either has proven to be unreliable in the past or may be expected to be so sometime in the future. Medium Grade.

5. *Standard & Poor's BB*. Investment desirability is limited. Operating deficits are possible under adverse economic conditions. Lower Medium Grade.
   Moody's Ba. An uncertain investment because operating strength cannot be predicted.

6. *Standard & Poor's B*.   Interest may not be paid during adverse times.
   Moody's B. Long-term obligations may not be met.

7. *Standard & Poor's CCC-CC*.   Speculative investments. Interest may only be paid when there is income.
   Moody's Caa. Bonds may be in default or interest and principal at risk.

8. *Standard & Poor's C*.   No interest being paid.
   Moody's Ca. Highly speculative. Often in default.

9. *Standard & Poor's DDD-D*.   All in default, with the rating corresponding to salvage value.
   Moody's C. Assumed to have no investment potential.

The Thirty Companies in the Dow Jones Industrial Average

1. Alcoa

2. Allied

3. American Brands

4. American Can

5. American Express

6. AT&T

7. Bethlehem Steel

8. E. I. Du Pont de Nemours

9. Eastman Kodak

10. Exxon

11. General Electric

12. General Foods

13. General Motors

14. Goodyear Tire & Rubber

15. IBM

16. Inco

17. International Harvester

18. International Paper

19. Merck

20. Minnesota Mining and Manufacturing

21. Owens-Illinois

22. Procter & Gamble

23. Sears Roebuck

24. Standard Oil (California)

25. Texaco

26. Union Carbide

27. United States Steel

28. United Technologies

29. Westinghouse Electric

30. F. W. Woolworth

The Eleven Stock Exchanges

All are registered with the Securities and Exchange Commission, with the exception of number eleven.

1. American

2. Boston

3. Chicago Board Options Exchange, Inc.

4. Cincinnati

5. Intermountain

6. Midwest

7. New York

8. Pacific

9. Philadelphia-Baltimore-Washington

10. Spokane

11. Honolulu

Ten Stock Market Don'ts

Authored by James B. Cloonan for the American Association of Individual Investors, a 70,000-member non-profit organization based in Chicago.

1. "Don't maintain an undiversified portfolio, one with fewer than seven stocks in it. You're better off with ten go-go stocks than one blue chip, as people who bought General Public Utilities found out when Three Mile Island happened. If you have less than $15,000, diversify through mutual funds."

2. "Don't buy preferred stocks, other than convertibles. They're good buys for corporations because of the dividend exclusion, but individuals get better yields from bonds."

3. "Don't move a substantial portion of your wealth into or out of the market at one time. Ease in, ease out."

4. "Don't buy common stocks with money you feel you will need in less than four years."

5. "Don't buy a stock that is getting a lot of play in the press."

6. "Don't buy stocks that are being pushed by a broker."

7. "Don't buy a stock that is included in the Fortune 500 or Standard & Poor's 500. The chances of such stocks being undervalued are virtually nil."

8. "Don't buy safe, low-risk stocks. Instead, buy growth stocks with some of your money and, for balance, put the rest into bonds or other minimum risk securities."

9. "Don't buy stocks for a year after a presidential inauguration. For some reason, the market almost always goes down in that period."

10. "Don't follow anyone's 'infallible system' for beating the market. Anyone with a system that really worked would never share it with others, because widespread use of it would cause the market to adjust and nullify it."

Nine Reasons the Stock Market Is So Volatile These Days

1. Computer technology is keeping investors better informed.

2. Computer technology is allowing brokerage houses to process more orders.

3. Stocks are being traded in bigger blocks because more institutions are amassing stock portfolios.

4. Pension fund managers are being pressured by their corporations to show short-term gains rather than long-term ones, forcing them to make rapid shifts in their portfolios.

5. Commissions have declined, leaving brokers and market makers less money with which to trade stocks to counter market trends.

6. The popularity of stock options and futures is encouraging more short selling and, as a result, prices are driven even higher in a bull market as investors rush to buy stocks.

7. Interest rates have been changing so rapidly that investors have been playing stocks and bonds against each other in hopes of finding the best deal.

8. An uncertain economy has left investors uneasy and unsure.

9. Investment advice has been irregular, with predictions of both a bull and a bear market.

Fourteen Sage Observations on the Stock Market

From Confusion de Confusiones, *written in 1688 by Joseph de la Vega about the Amsterdam stock market.*

1. *"Never give anyone the advice to buy or sell shares,* because where perspicacity is weakened, the most benevolent piece of advice can turn out badly."

2. "Take every gain without showing remorse about missed profits. . . ."

3. "Profits on the exchange are the treasures of goblins."

4. "Whoever wishes to win in this game must have patience and money, since the values are so little constant and the rumors so little founded on the truth."

5. ". . . these stock-exchange people are quite silly, full of instability, insanity, pride, and foolishness. They will sell without knowing the motive; they will buy without reason."

6. "He who makes it his business to watch these things conscientiously, without blind passion and irritating stubbornness, will hit upon the right thing innumerable times, though not always."

7. "The bulls are like the giraffe, which is scared by nothing, or like the magician of the Elector of Cologne, who in his mirror made the ladies appear much more beautiful than they were in reality. They love everything, they praise everything, they exaggerate everything."

8. "The bears, on the contrary, are completely ruled by fear, trepidation, and nervousness. Rabbits become elephants, brawls in a tavern become rebellions, faint shadows appear to them as signs of chaos."

9. ". . . excessively high values need not alarm you. There never lack princes of the exchange and kings of manipulations who are enamored of the shares. Be aware of the fact that there are as many speculators

as there are people, and that there will always be buyers who will free you from anxiety."

10. "The expectation of an event creates a much deeper impression upon the exchange than the event itself. When large dividends or rich imports are expected, shares will rise in price; but if the expectation becomes a reality, the shares often fall, for the joy over the favorable development and the jubilation over a lucky chance have abated in the meantime."

11. "... a 20 percent drop in the stock prices is not large enough to be considered a serious blow.... You do not have to despair and to bemoan your fate, for, as the price may drop 20 percent overnight, it may also rise 50 percent in the same period."

12. "When the speculators talk, they talk shares; when they run an errand, the shares make them do so; when they stand still, the shares act like a rein; when they look at something, it is shares that they see; when they think hard, the shares provide the content of their thoughts; if they eat, the shares are their food; if they meditate or study, they think of the shares; in their fever fantasies, they are occupied with shares; and even on the death bed, their last worries are the shares."

13. "... the speculator fights his own good sense, struggles against his own will, counteracts his own hope, acts against his own comfort, and is at odds with his own decisions."

14. "A witty man,. observing the business on the Exchange, ... remarked that the gamble on the Exchange was like death in that it made all people equal."

Source: Joseph de la Vega, "How to Beat the Stock Market—in the 1600s," in *The World of Business*, Volume II, eds. Edward C. Bursk, Donald T. Clark, and Ralph W. Hidy (New York: Simon and Schuster, Inc., 1962).

Eight Tax Shelters

1. *Oil and Gas Shelters.*   Mostly limited partnerships that allow you very large tax write-offs the first year and, if all goes well, generate sheltered income (you're allowed to deduct depletion allowances) when the wells begin producing.

2. *Real Estate.*   You can purchase real estate yourself for investment or you can purchase a limited partnership. Either way, the real estate should generate enough or nearly enough income to cover costs and allow you to deduct depreciation costs from your other income.

3. *Equipment Leasing.*   By purchasing a limited partnership in a leasing firm, you receive taxable income plus very high write-offs.

4. *Cattle Breeding.*   Cattle operators will purchase and take care of cattle for you. You are able to deduct all expenses plus depreciation and then receive taxable income through the sale of your herd's offspring.

5. *Municipal Bonds.*   You can purchase tax-free bonds individually or through a mutual fund, and all interest will be tax-free.

6. *Tax-Managed Funds.*   These are mutual funds that reinvest rather than pay dividends. You earn money when you sell your shares, which are then taxed at the lower capital-gains rate.

7. *IRAs.*   You are allowed to invest up to $2000 of your income a year and do not have to pay tax on it until you reach retirement age—a time when you will probably be in a lower tax bracket.

8. *Salary Reduction Plan.* Similar in principle to IRAs but worked out with your employer. The employer withholds a set percentage of your income (up to 10 percent), and it is available to you at retirement.

How to Win a Proxy Fight

1. Find a company which has high book value but is underpriced and possibly mismanaged.

2. Quietly buy enough shares on the open market to put you within striking distance of taking over the board.

3. Obtain a list of stockholders from the company, either by waiting until they voluntarily post it or by requesting it and filing suit for it if necessary.

4. Begin your campaign six to eight weeks before the annual meeting.

5. Clear all proxy solicitation efforts with the Securities and Exchange Commission.

6. Look for weak points in the corporate record.

7. Use a combination of phone calls and letters to reach stockholders, focusing on dissidents who hold large blocks of stock in their own names (rather than in the names of their brokers).

8. Be persuasive. Use effective direct-mail and phone solicitation techniques.

9. Stay in touch with stockholders until the last minute because they can always change their proxy votes if they wish.

10. Oversee the voting at the annual meeting.

Who You Don't Want
on Your Board

1. *Employees.*   They cannot take stands on tough issues if they are worried they may be fired as a result.

2. *Retired Employees.*   They may be inclined to promote business as it was, not business as it needs to be now and in the future.

3. *Professionals and Consultants.*   They cannot make corporate decisions and at the same time solicit your business as a client.

4. *Suppliers and Customers.*   As with professionals, these people are not disinterested bystanders. They cannot without bias make corporate decisions that may result in a monetary gain or loss for themselves.

5. *People in Your Industry.*   At some point, either now or in the future, they may be involved with your competition.

6. *Minority Stockholders.*   They are more likely to protect their investment than to vote in the best interests of the corporation.

7. *Friends.*   They may be too close to you to offer the kind of feedback you really need.

8. *Relatives.*   They may drag intrafamily squabbles into the boardroom.

9. *Spouses.*   They may not be especially qualified to take part in corporate decisions and therefore are little more than deadweight.

Adapted from Leon A. Danco and Donald J. Jonovic, *Outside Directors in the Family Owned Business: Why, When, Who and How* (Cleveland: The Center for Family Business, 1981).

7

BUSINESSES

Putting It All Together

Seven Comments by William Agee About Business and Finance

William Agee, former chairman of Bendix, has become famous for his rapid rise in the company, his relationship with Mary Cunningham (now his wife), and his unsuccessful attempt to take over Marietta Corporation. At various times he has been quoted as saying the following:

1. "You've got to begin with the basic tenet that the job of management is to maximize shareholder value."

2. "One of the problems with smokestack America is that managements haven't made a separation between what's in their best interests, as people who maybe have been in a single business twenty or thirty years, and what's in the shareholder's best interests. They rationalize that the two are the same."

3. "A new corporate CEO can't come into his job and simply continue churning out the hula hoops and widgets that built the enterprise."

4. "It's much better to be flexible about the businesses you are in than to go down the toilet managing a company that's stayed the same for thirty years."

5. "The problem any chief executive has is that you've got executives around you whispering in your ear to spend more money on operations they are associated with. As soon as the company gets some cash, they all come running in for a piece of the pie."

6. "I've learned you should never overestimate the rationality of some of your foes."

7. "Decide where you want to be and go there, always on your own terms. Always on your own terms."

Six Reasons to Deemphasize Capital Investment

1. Capital investment takes too long to produce immediate effects on the economy.

2. Capital investment may be overrated as the source of economic growth.

3. Capital investment has been emphasized to the detriment of other growth factors such as innovation, motivation, and leadership.

4. Capital investment may be an outdated concept. More capital investment does not always lead to economies of scale.

5. Capital investment does not guarantee productive investment.

6. Capital investment may gloss over the need for "disinvestment."

Adapted from C. Jackson Grayson, "Emphasizing Capital Investment Is a Mistake," *The Wall Street Journal*, October 11, 1982.

Twenty-two Signs That a Company Is in Trouble

1. Declining profitability
2. Declining net worth
3. Declining sales
4. Lack of growth
5. Increasing debt
6. Cash flow problems
7. Declining current assets to current liabilities ratio
8. Declining quick assets ratio
9. Increasing expense to sales ratios
10. Declining market share
11. Dividend cuts
12. Increasing inventories
13. Increasing product returns
14. Decreasing capital investment
15. Problems with banks and lenders—bad checks, late payments, loan defaults, loan turndowns
16. Problems with auditors—high turnover, warnings, reports of discrepancies
17. Management problems—high turnover, lack of planning
18. Milking subsidiaries—high cash flow to the main company
19. Too many new businesses started
20. Inattention to public relations

21. Increasing legal expenses
22. Large-scale stock sales by insiders

Fifteen Reasons Businesses Fail

Experts on bankruptcy, including owners of bankrupt businesses and their creditors, cite the following as common reasons for business failure.

According to the owners

1. Unfavorable economic conditions: 67.7 percent.
2. Undercapitalization: 48.2 percent.
3. Competition: 37.9 percent.
4. Personal and domestic problems: 35.1 percent.
5. Devaluation of assets: 31.6 percent.
6. Bad-debt losses: 29.8 percent.
7. Poor management: 28.2 percent.
8. Overhead expenses: 24.0 percent.
9. Bad location: 14.6 percent.
10. Speculative losses: 11.6 percent.
11. Trading area changes: 11.2 percent.
12. High interest payments: 11.1 percent.
13. Too rapid expansion: 10.5 percent.
14. Excessive use of credit: 9.5 percent.
15. Dishonesty and fraud: none.

According to the creditors

1. Poor management: 58.7 percent.

2. Dishonesty and fraud: 33.7 percent.

3. Undercapitalization: 32.9 percent.

4. Unfavorable economic conditions: 29.1 percent.

5. Personal and domestic problems: 28.1 percent.

6. Bad-debt losses: 17.6 percent.

7. Competition: 9.1 percent.

8. Overhead expenses: 8.9 percent.

9. Too rapid expansion: 7.2 percent.

10. Devaluation of assets: 5.8 percent.

11. Speculative losses: 5.8 percent.

12. Excessive use of credit: 3.9 percent.

13. Bad location: 2.7 percent.

14. High interest payments: 2.1 percent.

15. Trading area changes: 1.9 percent.

The Five Stages of a Corporate Turnaround

According to turnaround specialist Donald B. Bibeault, there are five stages in redirecting a failing company.

1. *Management Change Stage.* Since management problems are seen as the major cause of corporate decline, more often than not a board brings in new management to initiate the turnaround. Occasionally an insider—someone who has proved to be a good leader but has not been operating out of headquarters—can be found to take over, but in most cases an outsider—a growth-oriented executive, entrepreneur, or turnaround specialist—is asked to clean house and take over. He will immediately demonstrate his control by setting policy and giving orders. Initially his relationship with the company's employees will be good because they are eager for new leadership.

2. *The Evaluation Stage.* Very soon after moving in, the new CEO must size up the company's situation and problems and begin directing a new course.

3. *The Emergency Stage.* At this point, whatever drastic measures are needed to save the company will be made. Product lines will be pared down, unprofitable units sold, loans refinanced, and so on. The CEO's relationship with the company's employees will need work at this stage because they continue to function in their jobs but lack motivation.

4. *The Stabilization Stage.* "During stabilization, the emphasis shifts to a three-pronged strategy: first, concentrating on profitability in addition to cash flow; second, running existing operations better; and third, reposturing the company to provide a sound platform for medium-term growth." When things begin looking up, employee motivation will increase, and the new

CEO will be able to capitalize on this refound commitment.

5. *The Return-to-Normal-Growth Stage.* In many respects, the company has been reborn and can be run like a new company, positioning itself for fast growth and high profit margin. This momentum will spread to the employees, generating the sort of enthusiasm the company hasn't seen in years.

Source: Donald B. Bibeault, *Corporate Turnaround* (New York: McGraw-Hill, 1982).

The Seven Factors Considered Most Important in Turning Around a Company

Based on a survey of 81 CEOs of companies in turnaround:

1. Having absolute control: 24 percent.

2. Having tight control: 23 percent.

3. Better knowledge of the business: 17 percent.

4. Bringing about an attitude change: 12 percent.

5. Having visible leadership: 12 percent.

6. Having a more active board: 7 percent.

7. Having a strong financial officer: 4 percent.

Source: Donald B. Bibeault, *Corporate Turnaround* (New York: McGraw-Hill, 1982).

How to Acquire a Company Successfully

1. You must be willing to take risks.

2. You must want to be successful in that line of business.

3. You must know how to take charge quickly in that line of business or hire someone who does.

4. You must recognize that what is successful in one industry may not work in another.

5. You must be willing to incorporate the company's top management into your planning group.

How the Value of Closely Held Corporations Is Determined

A study based on 77 tax cases revealed that the following factors are used:

1. Expert testimony: 48 percent of the time.

2. Stock sales: 43 percent of the time.

3. Stock book value: 31 percent of the time.

4. Earnings history: 27 percent of the time.

5. Earnings power: 22 percent of the time.

6. Business type and history: 21 percent of the time.

7. Dividends: 16 percent of the time.

8. Asset value: 16 percent of the time.

9. Net working capital: 13 percent of the time.

10. Management type and quality: 12 percent of the time.

11. Marketability of stock: 8 percent of the time.

12. Economic prospects: 8 percent of the time.

13. Industry standing: 8 percent of the time.

14. Stock price comparisons: 6 percent of the time.

15. Dividends: 5 percent of the time.

16. Net worth growth: 5 percent of the time.

17. Goodwill is not used.

Source: S. J. Martin, "Factors the IRS and the Courts Are Using Today in Valuing Closely Held Shares," *Journal of Taxation*, February 1972.

Eleven Potential Problems in Family-Owned Businesses

1. *Conflicts of Interest.*   Family matters and goals may take precedence over business ones.

2. *Founder Dominance.*   As head of the family and the company, the founder may assume he knows what's best for everyone—both as relatives and as employees.

3. *Blocked Career Paths.*   Seldom can more than one or two members of the same generation hold the top spot. Therefore, most relatives are going to have to be content with lesser positions.

4. *Employee Relations.*   Rightly or wrongly, most non-family employees are going to assume they are being

discriminated against. They need to know what opportunities and benefits are available to them if they stay with the company.

5. *Succession.* A variety of problems can come up when the founder must designate a replacement. He may be reluctant to relinquish control and as a result, may name no one. Or an acceptable successor may not exist, either because there are no family members waiting in the wings or because no family member wants the job. Or a successor may be named but then opposed by the other relatives.

6. *Absentee Ownership.* Sometimes family members retain controlling interest in the company but spend their time pursuing other interests, rather than managing the business.

7. *Lack of Agreement.* Conflicts can arise when family members cannot agree on company goals yet do not want to relinquish control.

8. *Too Much Intimacy.* Family members usually know each other better than co-workers normally do and this can influence their perceptions of one another. They make evaluations based on reasons that extend beyond business competency.

9. *Lack of Objectivity.* Family members sometimes apply different criteria to judgment of each other than they would to that of outsiders.

10. *Sense of Family History.* Offspring who take over may be reluctant to make changes on the assumption that to do so would show disrespect to their predecessor.

11. *Power Struggles.* Fights within family-owned companies are often much nastier than in other companies because control of the business often means control of the family.

Eight Points to Consider When Deciding on Credit Policies

1. *Your Merchandise.*   It may be inefficient to offer credit for an inexpensive line but necessary for a higher priced one.

2. *Your Customers.*   If you deal with individuals or companies who like to pay bills on a monthly basis, who extend credit to their own customers, or who have widely fluctuating incomes which limit their cash purchases, you may find it necessary to offer credit. But if your customers are transients, you may risk a high percentage of bad debts and gain little in consumer loyalty if you do so.

3. *Your Competition.*   Others' credit policies may force you to offer something similar.

4. *Your Cash Flow.*   The smaller you are, the less likely it is that you will have the financial reserves to keep your inventory stocked while maintaining a large number of accounts receivable.

5. *Your Debt Obligations.*   You may be losing money if you extend credit at a rate lower than that of your own debt.

6. *Your Overhead.*   Accounts receivable cost money to process, and the amount of expense to you will depend on whether or not you are already paying for staff and equipment that can handle them.

7. *Your Consumer Relations.*   Maintaining charge accounts can help you acquire a loyal core of customers, the first ones you'll contact about sales and special promotions.

8. *Your Sales Strategy.*   You can use charge accounts to encourage customers to sample your merchandise

before paying for it. But at the same time, their returns are higher than those of cash customers.

Adapted from J. K. Lasser Tax Institute, *How to Run a Small Business*, 4th ed. (New York: McGraw-Hill, 1950, 1974).

Nine Kinds of Insurance a Company May Need

1. *Physical Damage.* This would include fire, flood, earthquake, and equipment damage.

2. *Leasehold Improvement Coverage.* This protects improvements made on leased property.

3. *Business Interruption.* This enables a company to meet its expenses when damage forces it to shut down temporarily.

4. *Casualty.* This would include personal liability, product liability, and others related to normal business operations.

5. *Personal Property.* This would cover damage to customers' property left in the care of the company.

6. *Crime.* This would include theft and employee dishonesty.

7. *Workmen's Compensation.* This covers the company's liability for workers, as outlined by individual states.

8. *Directors and Officers Liability.* This protects both company and individual against losses due to management decisions.

9. *Kidnap and Ransom.* This covers the costs of meeting kidnappers' demands when executives are abducted.

8

PLACES

Where to Go and Where It Happens

Comparative Housing Expenses in Seventeen Cities

Statistics gathered by Advance Mortgage Corporation of Detroit.

1.	St. Louis	24% of average household income
2.	Philadelphia	28%
3.	Cleveland	29%
4.	Houston	29%
5.	Minneapolis	32%
6.	Chicago	32%
7.	Denver	33%
8.	Miami	34%
9.	Boston	34%
10.	Phoenix	34%
11.	Detroit	37%
12.	Atlanta	37%

13. Washington, D.C. 39%

14. San Francisco   42%

15. New York   45%

16. Los Angeles   46%

17. San Diego   47%

Source: Robert Guenther, "Of the Big Cities, Philadelphia Has Most-Affordable Housing," *The Wall Street Journal*, February 9, 1983.

The Percentage of People Who Move When Their Companies Do

1. When the company moves from 5 to 10 miles away, 61 percent of the low-level staff and 88 percent of the high-level staff continue to work there.

2. When the company moves from 11 to 20 miles away, 55 percent of the low-level staff and 85 percent of the high-level staff continue to work there.

3. When the company moves from 21 to 40 miles away, 29 percent of the low-level staff and 69 percent of the high-level staff continue to work there.

4. When the company moves from 41 to 60 miles away, 18 percent of the low-level staff and 55 percent of the high-level staff continue to work there.

5. When the company moves over 60 miles away, 8 percent of the low-level staff and 64 percent of the high-level staff continue to work there.

Source: P. Friedly, *National Policy Responses to Urban Growth*, 1974 (Aldershot, Eng.: Gower Publishing Co., 1974).

Six Good Places to Locate a Business

1. *Austin, Texas.* The state capital, a high-tech center, and home of the University of Texas.

2. *Greenville-Spartanburg, South Carolina.* Two foreign consulates and more than fifty European corporate offices.

3. *Colorado Springs, Colorado.* A high-tech and military center.

4. *Tulsa, Oklahoma.* An oil center.

5. *Research Triangle, North Carolina.* Well over forty research and development firms located between Duke University, the University of North Carolina, and North Carolina State University.

6. *Las Vegas, Nevada.* Lots of tourist money and a good central location.

Source: Sam Allis, "Company Towns: Those Who Rate Cities as Business Sites Like Mid-Size Sun Belt Ones," *The Wall Street Journal*, March 14, 1980.

Nine Other Good Places to Locate a Business

1. Houston, Texas

2. Phoenix, Arizona

3. Fort Lauderdale, Florida

4. Tucson, Arizona

5. Albuquerque, New Mexico

6. Beaumont-Port Arthur-Orange, Texas

7. San Diego, California

8. El Paso, Texas

9. Columbus, Ohio

Source: Sam Allis, "Company Towns: Those Who Rate Cities as Business Sites Like Mid-Size Sun Belt Ones," *The Wall Street Journal*, March 14, 1980.

Seven European Opinions About Multinational Companies

Representatives from 111 multinational branch offices in the Netherlands, France, Germany, Belgium, and England were asked if they agreed with the following statements:

1. "Expatriate managers should be proficient in the host-country language": 100 percent agreed.

2. "Expatriate managers should have perfect knowledge of the host country's social characteristics": 92.5 percent agreed (ranging from 100 percent of the Flemish and French to 84.2 percent of the Germans).

3. "Expatriate managers should be of Western European ethnic origin": 89.3 percent agreed (ranging from 100 percent of the Flemish to 58 percent of the French).

4. "Expatriate managers should adhere to local managerial patterns of behavior": 87 percent agreed (ranging from 100 percent of the Flemish to 73.7 percent of the Germans).

5. "Expatriate managers should be thoroughly familiar with the culture of the host country": 86.1 percent agreed (ranging from 100 percent of the Flemish to 78.9 percent of the Germans).

6. "Expatriate managers should be thoroughly familiar with the history of the host country": 83.8 percent agreed (ranging from 100 percent of the Flemish to 75 percent of the French).

7. "All top managers of foreign subsidiaries should be host-country nationals": 63 percent agreed (ranging from 87.5 percent of the Dutch to 35.1 percent of the Germans).

Source: Yoram Zeira, "Ethnocentrism in Host-Country Organizations," *Business Horizons*, June 1979.

Thirteen Reasons the Japanese Excel at Production

1. Workers are valued as an essential part of the process.

2. Workers are trained to produce and expect high-quality products.

3. Products and production methods are carefully planned from the beginning, and everyone concerned, from engineers to sales managers, is consulted.

4. The necessary production equipment is created in-house rather than purchased, to maintain quality and meet the company's exact specifications.

5. Only high-quality materials are used, and suppliers are shown how to meet these standards.

6. Everything is kept spotless.

7. Equipment is regularly maintained and never over-loaded.

8. Machines are kept error-free through sophisticated monitoring systems.

9. Potential problems are anticipated and eliminated before they become crises.

10. Inventory is kept to a minimum by neither overstocking supplies nor overproducing goods.

11. The stated goal is "zero defects" and nothing less is acceptable.

12. Everyone, from suppliers and workers to consumers, is asked to give feedback.

13. Long-term relationships with both suppliers and consumers are sought and cultivated.

Adapted from Robert H. Hayes, "Why Japanese Factories Work," *Harvard Business Review*, July–August 1981.

9

WORKING

Reasons for Job Success and Failure

Six Jobs Now Held by More Women Than Men

1. Insurance adjusters, examiners, and investigators
2. Bill collectors
3. Checkers, examiners, and inspectors
4. Photographic process workers
5. Production-line assemblers
6. Real estate agents and brokers

Source: U.S. Labor Department, 1982.

Eight Reasons People Moonlight

1. To meet regular expenses: 53 percent of the black women, 37 percent of the black men, 32 percent of the white women, and 31 percent of the white men.
2. Because they enjoy the work: 19 percent of the white men, 16 percent of the white women, 13 percent of the black women, and 11 percent of the black men.

3. To have savings for the future: 18 percent of the black men, 12 percent of the white men, 8 percent of the black women, and 7 percent of the white women.

4. To be able to buy something special: 11 percent of the white women, 10 percent of the black women, 8 percent of the white men, and 1 percent of the black men.

5. To pay off debts: 11 percent of the black men, 7 percent of the white women, 7 percent of the white men, and 7 percent of the black women.

6. To gain experience: 9 percent of the white men, 7 percent of the white women, 6 percent of the black men, and 2 percent of the black women.

7. To help a friend or relative: 7 percent of the white women, 3 percent of the white men, 2 percent of the black women, and 1 percent of the black men.

8. Because they changed jobs: 3 percent of the black women and 2 percent of the white women.

Source: *Statistical Abstract of the United States*, 1982.

Why People Work More Than They Have To

1. *They enjoy it.* They are happy "workaholics" who love their jobs and love working at them. They are well adjusted and self-motivated.

2. *They need the money.* Emergencies do come up which require periods of extra effort. Most people can cope with overwork as long as they have a goal in mind and can imagine the time when things will be back to normal.

3. *Other people expect it.* Sometimes bosses or families put pressure on people to work harder. They may try for a while, but sooner or later they will burn out.

4. *They feel guilty.* Some people are afraid to enjoy themselves and think they must work all the time. They will keep up this pace until they can't (when health or other problems keep them from working) or until their values change.

5. *They are inefficient.* They work all the time because they can never get anything done. Either they need to be more organized or they must accept the fact that perhaps they honestly enjoy busy-work.

6. *They get high on stress.* Some people seem to be chemically addicted to the adrenaline that hard work and stress trigger. They suffer withdrawal symptoms when they can't work and seek out other obsessions (and/or substances) to fill the void.

7. *They want an escape.* Work can offer a way to avoid personal problems. This can be great short-term therapy (for coping with a failed marriage or the death of a loved one) but will lead to trouble over the long term.

8. *They have no other interests.* They work constantly because they have no other way to fill up time. This will be a problem if and when the job should end.

Thirteen Ways to Attract Good People to Your Company

1. Offer bonuses to join.

2. Guarantee future bonuses.

3. Give longer employment contracts.

4. Promise fast promotions.

5. Pay more than anyone else.

6. Send letters of invitation to promising college students.

7. Use a public relations campaign to enhance your image as an employer.

8. Offer training and managerial experience.

9. Offer control, responsibility, or a chance to develop a new product.

10. Draw college students through summer job programs.

11. Give good recruiting parties.

12. Use employees who hold similar jobs as recruiters.

13. Give chances to socialize with top management.

How Often Managers
Make Career Moves

Based on a survey of 1,191 men.

1. Every three to four years: 22.5 percent.

2. Every two to three years: 21 percent.

3. Every four to five years: 14.5 percent.

4. Every five to six years: 10 percent.

5. Every six to seven years: 8 percent.

6. Every one to two years: 5.4 percent.

7. Every seven to eight years: 4.6 percent.

8. Every eight to nine years: 3 percent.

9. Every twelve or more years: 3 percent.

10. Every nine to ten years: 3 percent.

11. Every ten to eleven years: 3 percent.

12. Every eleven to twelve years: 2 percent.

Source: John F. Veiga, "Do Managers on the Move Get Anywhere?" *Harvard Business Review*, March–April 1981.

Seven Factors That Increase Managerial Commitment to the Organization

Listed in order of importance.

1. Managers feel that their jobs are considered important by others.

2. The organization has met managers' initial expectations.

3. Managers are working in a friendly, close-knit group.

4. During their first year with the organization, managers worked with others who had a positive attitude about their workplace.

5. Managers are currently working with others who have a positive attitude about their workplace.

6. Managers are expected to feel committed to the organization.

7. Managers had challenging work to do in their first year with the organization.

Adapted from Bruce Buchanan, "Building Organizational Commitment: The Socialization of Managers in Work Organizations," *Administrative Science Quarterly*, December 1974.

What It Takes to Get Ahead

From a Wall Street Journal/Gallup Organization poll of chief executives in various-sized companies. Percentages reflect multiple answers from many of the respondents.

In Large Companies

Based on the answers given by CEOs of 282 of the country's largest corporations, including 102 Fortune 500 firms.

1. Integrity: 36 percent.

2. The ability to get along with others: 32 percent.

3. Industriousness: 25 percent.

4. Intelligence: 25 percent.

5. Knowledge of business: 23 percent.

6. Leadership: 15 percent.

7. Technical experience: 14 percent.

8. Education: 5 percent.

In Medium-Sized Companies

Based on the answers given by CEOs of 300 medium-sized firms.

1. The ability to get along with others: 36 percent.

2. Integrity: 27 percent.

3. Knowledge of business: 25 percent.

4. Industriousness: 23 percent.

5. Technical experience: 14 percent.

6. Intelligence: 14 percent.

7. Leadership: 12 percent.

8. Education: 7 percent.

In Small Companies

Based on the answers given by owners of 200 small firms.

1. The ability to get along with others: 34 percent.

2. Integrity: 24 percent.

3. Industriousness: 24 percent.

4. Knowledge of business: 24 percent.

5. Intelligence: 10 percent.

6. Leadership: 10 percent.

7. Technical experience: 6 percent.

8. Education: 1 percent.

Source: Frank Allen, "Bosses List Main Strengths, Flaws Determining Potential of Managers," *The Wall Street Journal*, November 14, 1980.

P. T. Barnum's Guide
to Success

1. "The road to wealth...consists simply in expending less than we earn..."

2. "The safest plan, and the one most sure of success for the young man starting in life, is to select the vocation which is most congenial to his tastes."

3. "Unless a man enters upon the vocation intended for him by nature, and best suited to his peculiar genius, he cannot succeed."

4. "Young men starting in life should avoid running into debt.... There is no greater mistake than when a young man believes he will succeed with borrowed money."

5. "Whatever you do, do it with all your might. Work at it, if necessary, early and late, in season and out of season, not leaving a stone unturned, and never deferring for a single hour that which can be done just as well now."

6. "The eye of the employer is often worth more than the hands of a dozen employees."

7. "Men engaging employees should be careful to get the best. Understand, you cannot have too good tools to work with, and there is no tool you should be so particular about as *living* tools."

8. "If you get a good [employee], it is better to keep him, than keep changing. He learns something every day, and you are benefited by the experience he acquires.... [But] if, as he gets more valuable, he demands an exorbitant increase in salary, on the supposition that you can't do without him, let him go."

9. "An important element in an employee is the brain."

10. "Do not scatter your powers. Engage in one kind of business only, and stick to it faithfully until you suc-

ceed or until your experience shows that you should abandon it."

11. "Men should be systematic in their business. A person who does business by rule, having a time and place for everything, doing his work promptly, will accomplish twice as much and with half the trouble of him who does it carelessly and slipshod."

12. "Always take a trustworthy newspaper, and thus keep thoroughly posted in regard to the transactions of the world. He who is without a newspaper is cut off from his species."

13. "Your object in advertising is to make the public understand what you have to sell, and if you have not the pluck to keep advertising, until you have imparted that information, all the money you have spent is lost."

14. "Politeness and civility are the best capital ever invested in business."

Source: P. T. Barnum, *Dollars and Sense or How to Get On* (New York: Henry S. Allen, 1890).

Nineteen Unusual Perquisites and Benefits Companies Offer

1. Low-interest college tuition loans for employees' children.

2. In-house computer stores.

3. No-interest loans to buy home computers.

4. In-house car wash and auto repair service.

5. In-house divorce counseling.

6. Time off for Christmas shopping.

7. Free tax advice and preparation.

8. Reimbursement of adoption expenses.

9. Corporate gardens.

10. In-house day-care centers.

11. Subsidized family day-care homes that operate in the evenings and on weekends.

12. Reimbursement of child-care expenses.

13. In-house parenting programs.

14. In-house antismoking programs.

15. Corporate-owned vacation homes.

16. Monetary gifts for getting married, having a child, and graduating a child from high school.

17. In-house clubs for after-hours socializing.

18. College extension courses.

19. Noncredit enrichment courses and lunchtime lectures.

Eight Causes of Job Stress

According to John R.P. French, Jr., and Robert D. Caplan, psychologists at the University of Michigan's Institute for Social Research, the following cause job stress:

1. *Role Ambiguity.*   Not having enough information about your job.

2. *Role Conflict.*   Having to carry out conflicting demands.

3. *Role Overload.*   Having to work on too many projects at once and having to work beyond your "skills, abilities, and knowledge."

4. *Organizational Territoriality.*   Having to work where you don't feel you belong.

5. *Responsibility for People.*   Having too little or too much.

6. *Poor Relations with Others.*   Poor communication, which results in too little trust and support from others.

7. *Participation.*   Being excluded from decision making.

8. *Occupational Differences.*   Factors inherent in the job which create stress.

Source: John R.P. French, Jr., and Robert D. Caplan, "Organizational Stress and Individual Strain," in *The Failure of Success*, ed. Alfred Marrow (New York: AMACOM, 1972).

Ten Causes of Personal Failure

1. *Blaming Others.*   If we don't accept responsibility for failure, we can't learn from our mistakes.

2. *Blaming Ourselves.*   If we assume we can do no right, we have little incentive to strive for anything.

3. *Having No Goals.*   Without goals, our efforts lead us nowhere.

4. *Having the Wrong Goals.*   Without the right goals, our efforts take us in the wrong direction and keep us too busy to change course.

5. *Taking Shortcuts.*   Rarely can anything really worthwhile be achieved quickly and easily.

6. *Taking Too Long.*   Putting off success or not realizing when we have reached it can undermine all of our hard work.

7. *Neglecting Details.*   A grand plan can be undone when we forget or overlook all the loose ends and nuances that make it work.

8. *Quitting Too Soon.*   Sometimes we lose perspective when we are in the middle of a project and quit when we are tired, even though we have almost reached our goal.

9. *Clinging to the Past.*   Good or bad, the past stays with many of us because we know it; the unknown seems riskier. But we cannot make progress unless we go forward.

10. *Taking Success for Granted.*   Sometimes we think we have reached our goals only to fall short or to lose what we briefly held. Success is an ongoing process and cannot be taken for granted.

Adapted from pages 48–63 of *The Road to Successful Living*, by Louis Binstock (New York: Simon and Schuster, Inc., 1958).

Five Reasons People End Up in the Wrong Jobs

Based on a survey of 1,189 people.

1. They follow the advice of others instead of their own instincts: 30 percent.

2. They blind themselves to what the job will really be like: 25 percent.

3. They assume they can live with a lower salary than they're used to: 20 percent.

4. They do not check out potential problems and issues during the interview: 15 percent.

5. They impulsively grab the first job that comes along: 10 percent.

Source: Marilyn Moats Kennedy, *Career Knockouts: How to Battle Back* (Chicago: Follett Publishing Co., 1980).

How to Know If Your Job Is Safe After a Merger

1. The acquiring company will want you to stay if you have skills it needs.

2. The acquiring company will want you to stay if you play an important role in a profitable operation.

3. The acquiring company will not want you to stay if you aren't willing to work with it and use its methods.

4. The acquiring company will not need you if reorganization eliminates your areas of responsibility.

5. The acquiring company will want you to stay if you have desirable contacts or essential knowledge about operations or production.

6. The acquiring company may not want to keep you if you earn more than its employees do for the same job.

7. The acquiring company may not want to keep you if your salary is higher than the industry average for your position.

8. The acquiring company will not need you if your job merely duplicates functions already handled by its staff.

9. The acquiring company will not want you if you openly and strenuously fought against the merger.

10. The acquiring company may feel you are expendable if you hold a staff position.

11. The acquiring company may have little interest in keeping you if you are too old or too entrenched in the company to be hired by a competitor.

Adapted from John L. Handy, "How to Face Being Taken Over," *Harvard Business Review*, November–December 1969.

Sixteen Signs That Your Job Could Be in Trouble

1. No one stops by your desk to chat anymore, and you haven't been invited to a co-worker's house for dinner in months.

2. No one seems to want to have lunch with you anymore.

3. You're being included in fewer meetings than you used to be.

4. You're being offered assignments you can't possibly accept because of personal or professional conflicts which are common knowledge.

5. No one checks in with you before new people are hired in your department.

6. You're not getting as many memos as you once did.

7. New people are getting promotions and raises faster than you are.

8. Outside management consultants have been asking about your job responsibilities but haven't been asking others about theirs.

9. The personnel department wants you to take a series of tests that no one else is taking.

10. People keep telling you about other jobs you'd be great at.

11. You are overdue for a job evaluation session, or when you have one, no one asks you about your career plans.

12. You are being volunteered for projects that keep you busy in the community and out of your office.

13. New people are being brought in to help you out with projects you've been working on for months.

14. Organizational or policy changes catch you by surprise.

15. You've been asked to share your secretary with someone.

16. You've been told you need a vacation.

Twenty-three Effects of Unemployment

1. Anxiety

2. Divorce

3. Aging

4. Hopelessness

5. Anger

6. Frustration

7. Fear

8. Depression

9. Alcoholism

10. Violence

11. Mental illness

12. Unhappy children

13. Desperation

14. Suicide

15. Child abuse

16. High blood pressure

17. Insomnia

18. Unhappy spouses

19. Demoralization

20. Loss of self-esteem

21. Sexual problems

22. Psychosomatic illness

23. Defensiveness

Ten Kinds of Résumés

1. *Basic*.   Good for those with little work experience. Includes personal information, objectives, school and job backgrounds, military service record, and hobbies worth mentioning.

2. *Chronological*.   Good for those with job experience. Includes job history (with most recent employer given first and so on down to initial employer), school background, professional and community background, hobbies worth mentioning, and personal information.

3. *Chronological with Summary*.   A chronological résumé with qualifications elaborated on a separate page.

4. *Functional*.   Good for those with strong experience but an irregular work history. Includes employment information broken down according to skills used.

5. *Functional by Company*.   Differs from the functional résumé only in that companys worked for are first identified and then broken down according to skills used.

6. *Accomplishment*.   Similar to a functional résumé but does not mention dates. Good for older workers or those who have been out of the labor market for a long time.

7. *Professional*.   Good for those in fields requiring extensive preparation. Includes qualifications and academic and professional training.

8. *Narrative*.   Good for those who can write well and need flexibility in telling about themselves. Done in a modified essay form.

9. *Creative*.   Good for those looking for work in artistic or other creative fields. Includes imaginative or eye-catching organization, graphics, language, and so on.

10. *Harvard*.   Good for those who want to indicate a high-class business background. Its form ("narrow margins and long, rather informal paragraphs" with dense writing) brings about an "immediate association by sophisticated readers with the Harvard Graduate School of Business Administration."

Adapted from Burdette E. Bostwick, *Résumé Writing: A Comprehensive How-to-Do-It Guide* (New York: John Wiley & Sons, 1976).

Nine Kinds of Résumé Fraud

1. Listing college and graduate degrees that came from unaccredited schools or diploma mills.

2. Claiming a degree from a school attended for only a short period of time.

3. Inflating the level of education.

4. Listing schools never attended.

5. Using falsified school records.

6. Incorrectly stating military record.

7. Exaggerating past job responsibilities.

8. Giving distorted salary figures from previous jobs.

9. Neglecting to list jobs held only briefly or fired from.

Six Factors That Contribute to Your Image

1. *Clothes*.   People make assumptions about your position, your family background, and your education based on what they see you wearing. The trick is to dress the way you want to be seen, not according to your own tastes or preferences.

2. *Manners.* People make assumptions about your upbringing, your worldliness, and your feelings for them based on what they see you doing or not doing in social situations. You must realize not only that manners are important, but also that you probably don't know everything there is to know on the subject and should do some research.

3. *Speech.* What you say and the way you say it can trigger prejudice against you faster than anything else you do. Poor grammar will reflect not only on your education, but also—perhaps unfairly—on your intelligence. A thick accent will link you to all the negative stereotypes people form about ethnic groups and regions. More often than not, such problems need the help of a professional to be corrected.

4. *Voice.* When you speak in an unnatural voice, you not only hurt your vocal cords, but also influence people's impression of you. When you speak in a high, thin voice or a low, gravelly voice, you project an image that may undercut what you are trying to say. You may need the services of a voice coach who can show you how to speak in a comfortable, easy-to-listen-to manner.

5. *Teeth.* Cosmetic dentists are now suggesting that people judge you by what they see in your mouth. Big canine teeth can make you look overly aggressive, and buck teeth can make you look stupid. By having such problems corrected, you will be able to project a more accurate and pleasing image.

6. *Weight.* Unfortunately, overweight people are often discriminated against at work. People expect fast-trackers to have a lean and hungry look. And they expect well-rounded executives to take care of their

bodies and their health as well as they take care of
business. Therefore, if for no other reason than your
career, you must be conscientious about exercise and
diet.

Eight Ways in Which Luck Becomes a Factor in Business

1. Through a chance meeting with someone who later
   plays an important part in business negotiations (i.e.,
   getting stranded on an airplane with a person who turns
   out to be CEO of a company you want to acquire).

2. Through a direction change because a desired choice
   is unexpectedly unavailable (e.g., being forced to
   choose another office location because the one you
   wanted was mistakenly leased to someone else).

3. Through a direction change because of an unexpected
   social or political change (e.g., manufacturing products
   tied in with the Olympics only to see the games boy-
   cotted).

4. Through a direction change because of an unexpected
   natural disaster (e.g., losing a new building during a
   freak tornado).

5. Through a direction change because of an unexpected
   personal development (e.g., making a major professional commitment just before your spouse is killed in
   a plane crash, leaving you with two small children to
   take care of).

6. Through a direction change because of an unexpected
   career development (e.g., being asked to take on a new

assignment which proves more interesting and satis-
fying than your present activities).

7. Through being in the right place at the right time (e.g.,
   overhearing the competition discussing a new campaign in the men's room of an obscure little restaurant
   you've never been to before).

8. Through a minor detour with major consequences (e.g.,
   missing a meeting because your flight was late only to
   find out in the newspapers the next day that the man
   you were to negotiate with is being charged with
   embezzlement).

What We Lose in Retirement

1. *A Sense of Belonging to a Group.*   For most of us,
   the strongest group identification we will ever have is
   with our co-workers. To develop that closeness with
   another group takes time.

2. *A Sense of Purpose.*   Most of us channel our personal
   goals into the corporation: when business is good, we
   feel a sense of accomplishment. After a lifetime of
   commitment to an organization, or at least to the business community in general, we may feel a tremendous
   void upon retiring.

3. *Power and Influence.*   Relatively few of us possess
   personal power—power divorced from our positions
   and the resources we command and have access to.
   Without those to lend us credibility, we feel naked.

4. *Schedules.*   A job defines our day. Leisure time can
   be a terrible burden if we have nothing with which to
   fill it.

5. *A Sense of Territory.* At work most of us have our own personal space—an office, a desk, a locker—something that is ours alone. At home we may have to share with others, and this becomes most evident when we no longer have a place of our own to go to every day.

6. *A Sense of Contribution to the Home.* Many of us depend on a job to bolster our self-images. We are providing for our families. In retirement we may feel unsure of our role in the household.

7. *An Opportunity for Stimulation.* At work we learn new things and are exposed to new ideas. In retirement we may have no source of information or no person with similar experience to talk to.

Adapted from Leland P. Bradford, "Can You Survive Your Retirement?" *Harvard Business Review*, November–December 1979.

Five Retirement Guidelines

According to Mortimer Feinberg, chairman of BFS Psychological Associates, a New York consulting firm, and Aaron Levenstein, professor of management at Baruch College, these are five ways to prepare for retirement:

1. *Work with and prepare your successor.* It will help you acknowledge your coming retirement, will serve as a transition period, and will enhance your record at the company.

2. *Think of ways to use your business experience elsewhere.* Perhaps you can try a new occupation, become a consultant or a volunteer.

3. *"Develop outside interests and think of retirement as an opportunity to devote yourself to them."* By broadening your view of life and realizing that work need not be your only source of satisfaction, you'll be able to view retirement positively.

4. *Be prepared to readjust your business relationships.* After retirement, you may not find it comfortable or wise to stay in touch with those at work except on a social basis when they take the initiative.

5. *Find community outlets for your leadership abilities.* Increase the time you spend on volunteer activities and serve on various community boards.

Adapted from Mortimer R. Feinberg and Aaron Levenstein, "Retirement as the Pinnacle of Your Career," *The Wall Street Journal*, November 23, 1981.

10

LIFESTYLE

After-Hours Tips and Pursuits

How Workers Want Companies to Promote
Good Family
Relationships

Percentages reflect multiple answers by many of the respondents.

1. More flexible working hours: 54 percent.

2. Sick leave when family members are sick: 37 percent.

3. Four-day work weeks: 31 percent.

4. On-site day-care facilities: 28 percent.

5. Freedom to refuse overtime: 21 percent.

6. Part-time work: 19 percent.

7. Fewer relocations: 19 percent.

8. On-site family counseling: 18 percent.

9. Opportunity to share jobs with spouses: 12 percent.

10. Better maternity leave policies: 9 percent.

Source: The Gallup Organization poll, March 1980.

Eight Things Executive Wives Get

The Wall Street Journal *and The Gallup Organization surveyed 476 women—approximately "20 percent of all wives of top executives in the 1,300 largest U.S. companies"—and found that they had the following*:

1. Country club membership	79 percent
2. Overseas vacation in past year	53 percent
3. Summer, winter, or vacation home	53 percent
4. Swimming pool	35 percent
5. Sleep-in boat	11 percent
6. Live-in domestic help	10 percent
7. Tennis court	9 percent
8. Airplane	7 percent

Source. *The Wall Street Journal*, December 15, 1981.

Four Kinds of Corporate Husbands

According to Maryanne Vandervelde, president of Pioneer Management, a Seattle-based consulting firm, corporate husbands come in four varieties:

1. *The Achiever Obstructionist.* Approximately 50 percent of all corporate husbands. He gives lip service to his wife's career, but he isn't truly supportive because he expects her to do everything at home as well. But he does provide money, companionship, and accompaniment to parties.

2. *The Achiever Facilitator.* Perhaps 25 percent of all corporate husbands. He appreciates his wife's career and is willing to help her achieve success in it by being a friend and a domestic partner.

3. *The Non-Achiever Facilitator.* Around 20 percent of all corporate husbands. His wife's career is dominant and he works around it by running the home, adapting his career, and listening to her problems.

4. *The Non-Achiever Obstructionist.* Only about 5 percent of all corporate husbands. He isn't successful himself and undermines his wife as well. She might stay with him only because of the children or for religious reasons.

Source: Maryanne Vandervelde, "Corporate Husbands," *The Wall Street Journal*, September 29, 1980.

Twelve Options for Two-Career Couples When One Person Has to Relocate

1. Negotiate with your respective companies for simultaneous relocation.

2. Approach the relocating person's company with a list of conditions and acceptable options (e.g., you'll relocate if your husband or wife can find another job; you'll relocate in two years; and so on).

3. Defer to the needs of the person with the most specialized job on the assumption that he or she has the fewest job options.

4. Make a checklist of career plans and needs for each of you and work out a compromise.

5. Alternate taking advantage of career opportunities, with the understanding that certain stages in each career are more critical than others.

6. Work for the same company, asking for simultaneous transfers.

7. Go into business together, or at least work in dovetailing fields.

8. Subordinate one career to the other.

9. Move to a city halfway between the new location and the old one, so each of you can commute.

10. Have one of you commute between the new location and the old one.

11. Temporarily go in separate directions.

12. Forego traditional roles and have the husband stay home.

Adapted from Cathleen E. Maynard and Robert A. Zawacki, "Mobility and the Dual-Career Couple," *Personnel Journal*, July 1979.

Nineteen Kinds of Airline Meals You Can Order

Most airlines will try to meet your special dietary needs or preferences if you give them from four to twenty-four hours' notice before the flight. Some of the possibilities are:

1. *Strained.* Usually prepared for children under two years of age, this menu might also be appropriate for adults who are unable to chew their foods.

2. *Children's.* Hot dogs, spaghetti, and the like.

3. *Bland.* No nuts or fried, spicy, or gas-producing foods.

4. *Diabetic.* No foods with sugar, honey, or corn syrup.

5. *Low Sodium.* No foods with salt added or used in the processing.

6. *Lactose Restricted.* No milk or milk products.

7. *Gluten-Free.* Nothing made from wheat, rye, oats, barley or buckwheat.

8. *Low Cholesterol.* No fatty foods, including whole milk, cream, butter, and egg yolks.

9. *Low Fat.* Similar to low cholesterol but also excludes vegetables with rich sauces and ones cooked with fats.

10. *High Protein.* Includes foods with a high ratio of protein to fat and carbohydrate.

11. *Weight Watchers.* Menus approved by Weight Watchers International.

12. *Vegetarian.* No foods from animal sources.

13. *Lacto-Ovo Vegetarian.* Vegetarian that includes milk and eggs.

14. *Oriental*. Includes oriental vegetables and certain cooking styles.

15. *Hindu*.   No beef or veal.

16. *Kosher*. Prepared by an approved caterer and includes no pork, shellfish, or meat and dairy products that have been prepared together.

17. *Muslim*.   No pork or shellfish. ·

18. *Soul Food*.   Includes highly spiced home-style cooking.

19. *Mormon*.   No caffeine or alcoholic products used in preparation.

ABOUT THE AUTHOR

Suzanne Lainson writes regularly for many magazines. She has researched thousands of titles and interviewed hundreds of people for CRASH COURSE. She lives in Colorado.

By the year 2000, 2 out of 3 Americans could be illiterate.

It's true.

Today, 75 million adults...about one American in three, can't read adequately. And by the year 2000, U.S. News & World Report envisions an America with a literacy rate of only 30%.

Before that America comes to be, you can stop it...by joining the fight against illiteracy today.

Call the Coalition for Literacy at toll-free **1-800-228-8813** and volunteer.

**Volunteer
Against Illiteracy.
The only degree you need
is a degree of caring.**

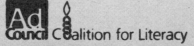 Ad Council Coalition for Literacy

LV-2